i

Private Ray Paine, 70th Northamptonshire Regt August 1942

From Mortar To Mortar

– Ray Paine –

www.fast-print.net/store.php

FROM MORTAR TO MORTAR
Copyright © Ray Paine 2013

A catalogue record for this book is available from the British Library

ISBN 978-178035-668-6

Front and back cover design by Stuart Paine and Rosie Shorter

First published 2013 by FASTPRINT PUBLISHING, Peterborough, England.

This book is dedicated to my wife Audrey and my best friend, Charlie Smith.

Contents

Photographs

Frontispiece :
Private Ray Paine, 70th Northamptonshire Regt August 1942

Between pages 44 and 51 :

Ray in mortar pit with 3" mortar, Barnstorf   11 April 1945
Charlie Smith, Ray's best friend
Ray in wagon, Barnstorf 9 April 1945
Mortar team Barnstorf April 1945
Ray in Lengerich 9 May 1945
Ray in Belgium October 1945
Charlie and Mac on train
Ray in Hadera, Palestine late 1945
Bremen airfield   26 April 1945
Ray bricklaying
Ray and Audrey's wedding 26 June 1948

Introduction

My father never used to talk about the war when we were young. I knew he had fought in the war but I didn't know what he did. "Did you kill anyone during the war, Dad?" I asked on several occasions but he would not be drawn. "It was kill or be killed," he used to say. Then when he finally did tell us about it he talked about it constantly - as though the experience had to remain dormant for forty years before he finally came to terms with it and could share it with others.

His obvious moment of fame and glory was his landing on Sword Beach on D-Day aged twenty-one - at that critical moment probably with a very short life expectancy. Although not mentioned in his memoirs, I clearly remember my father relating how the commanding officers cut a pack of cards to decide where their men would be positioned in the landing craft as they approached the beaches. He said that his C.O. cut a low card and so he was at the back. This tale may of course be anecdotal, but I have often related it to demonstrate how my sisters and I probably owe our existence to the four of clubs.

My father was always a hero to me. He used to play cricket for Arthingworth, a small rural village a few miles from Desborough where we lived. Later on he played for Desborough. He was a bowler and used to come in to bat at number 10 or 11, but he was so good at not getting out that one season he was top of the batting averages. His highest score was sixty-nine which is quite impressive for a bowler. He was always coming home with bruises on his legs and on one occasion with a black eye after being hit by a short ball.

In the 1970s I was at a posh dinner party in North London with my wife Carol and her fellow fashion designers. The conversation got around to what our fathers did during the war. As we went round the table, a clear pattern began to emerge of generals, diplomats and ambassadors, men who probably spent most of their war years a long way from the action. When it came round to me and I said that my father had landed on Sword Beach on D-Day, there was a murmur of admiration from all present at the significance of this and I suddenly felt very proud of what my father had done.

The whole family took Ray back to Normandy in 1990, the first time he had returned, and we visited Arromanches, the Pegasus Bridge and the war cemeteries. We tried to find the exact spot where he landed at Lion-sur-Mer on D-Day, but since he had only spent a very short time there on his first visit we were unsuccessful and satisfied ourselves with a photograph of him sitting on a bench on the sea wall. At the Pegasus Bridge café, my father introduced himself to Arlette Gondrée, the owner, who had been there when the first parachutists landed. I remember the warm welcome he received and the shyness he displayed, as though awe-stricken to meet her. Later I was standing on the bridge fifty yards away as he came out of the café, when a sudden gust of wind blew over a metal stand of postcards, scattering them all over the road. He rushed to help pick them up. I suddenly had a fear of him having survived several years of war here being knocked down by a car forty years later, and ran back quickly to usher him away. My father corresponded with Arlette after this visit and I believe she visited Desborough as a guest of honour on at least one occasion.

My father made several further trips to northern France over a number of years and on one visit in 1994 was presented with a Jubilee Medal by the President of the Normandy Regional Council in recognition of his role in the D-Day landings and the liberation of Normandy.

My father joined the Normandy Veterans' Association and regularly used to attend their meetings. He said that at one meeting an application to join had been received from a German living in England. There appeared to be nothing in the rules to prevent a German joining – after all he was a bona fide Normandy veteran. But there was some dissent and a split in the members. I was proud that my father was on the side of those who were willing to forgive and allow him to join, although I do not know the outcome.

Recently I have taken up climbing the Scottish mountains. On one trip I had decided to climb Beinn Resipol in honour of my father's ascent during his military training, and also so that I could photograph it and talk to him about it before he forgot its importance, or indeed who I was. The mountain is 2772 feet high and a long way from anywhere on the Ardnamurchan peninsula, and I misjudged the time and weather, arriving there in mid-afternoon in torrential rain. I was determined to climb it though and set off. The weather was dreadful, I got lost in thick mist and it began to get dark. I really should have turned back much sooner than I did, but it was my father's mountain and I continued recklessly upwards until I was completely lost, before descending in complete darkness. I would not have liked to run down the mountain as my father had to in 1943. A framed photograph of the mountain is now on the wall in his room. I did eventually climb it in 2012 with my son, Stuart, and his fiancée Rosie. So now three generations of Paines have stood on that remote summit.

Sadly at the time of writing, my father is in a care home, aged ninety and suffering from Alzheimers. Although a number of times in the book he wrote about things that he promised never to forget, he now has done. My sister Barbara wrote a poem about him which is pinned to the wall in his room.

This book is my father's account of his war years – the training in Scotland, climbing Beinn Resipol, the landing on D-Day and the campaign across northern Europe and into Germany. I have tried to keep as much of it as possible in his own words, but have corrected some of the grammar and reworded occasionally for clarity. Some of the background information on the wider war theatre has no doubt been gleaned from other sources to maintain the flow of the narrative where his memory was deficient and to put his personal experiences into context. My special thanks go to Patrick Delaforce, author of Monty's Ironsides, published by Alan Sutton. My father lent photographs and provided some quotes for his book. In later correspondence between Patrick and me he provided me with this quote : "The 3rd British Division were magnificent. My Division (11th Armoured) fought alongside the 3rd British in Normandy and in the winter of 1944 in Holland. Best wishes to your father."

On returning from active service, my father married Audrey Crick of 6 Dunkirk Avenue, Desborough in 1948. They had lived next door to each other in Queen Street when they were young. Barbara, Jennifer and I were born in the 1950s and we all lived at 35 Braybrooke Road. Just after the birth of Jennifer, Ray contracted acute lupus erythematosus which would probably have killed him were it not for the newly-invented drug Cortizone. My father worked as a bricklayer and builder for most of his life and finally retired in 1988. This explains the title of the book – his journey from firing mortars in the war to laying mortar for bricks.

This is his story.
Dave Paine 2013

FROM MORTAR TO MORTAR

– Ray Paine –

Chapter One
Call-Up and Training

I was working with Bill Pateman on an air-raid shelter in King Street, Desborough opposite where Toones Factory used to be. Being a little older than me he had his papers to call him for a medical prior to being called up for the forces. When Bill had left and joined the Royal Marine Commandos I knew it would not be long before I would be called for a medical, as we were both in the same class at the Church School, and sure enough at the end of May 1942 I had my papers come through the post to go to Dover Hall, Northampton, for a medical test etc.

On the day I travelled by train to Market Harborough and then through to Northampton Castle Station, to find Dover Hall just over the bridge from the station. In the hall were different doctors who were either prodding us, or tapping with a little hammer, or making us drop our trousers and telling us to cough! One of them was my own doctor, Dr. Gibbons, who said to me, "Bad luck, you're A1." While I was there I tried to get into the R.A.F. who used bricklayers on airfields but was told there were no vacancies, so that was knocked on the head. The Royal Marines were there recruiting. The sergeant looked me up and down and said, "We need six-footers like you." I enquired what it entailed, and he started to mention ships and the Navy, but I had quickly moved on to the next recruitment booth. Here they told me that they were starting a new 70th Battalion Northants Regiment at No.2 I.T.C. in Norwich on the second week in August. "Are you interested?" I said "Yes, OK." From then on I signed forms and then took the oath that I would be faithful and bear true allegiance to His Majesty King George the Sixth etc. etc. I was then paid the King's shilling, but by the time I joined it had gone up to five shillings.

I came out of Dover Hall with everything sealed, signed and a volunteer for the Army, and I must admit feeling quite chuffed! (So much for never volunteering for anything). Arriving home and telling Mother what I had done did not go down too well and it took her a little time to get used to her son who would be in the Army in five or six weeks' time.

I finished work two weeks before the time came round to join the Army and spent some days in London, which I liked to do, and saw one or two films and visited the War Museum. I called up some friends in East Ham who would always put me up for the night.

But, as always time slipped by and the two weeks were over. The Monday morning arrived when it was time to say goodbye to Mum and Dad and leave home. Travelling to Kettering on the bus, it began to sink in that I was now on my own and wondering what was about to happen in the near future.

Walking from the bus depot down to the station and showing my rail pass, I was told to go to the left, and there stood the train for Cambridge. I boarded the train and had just put my case on the luggage rack when another man joined me and sat opposite next to the window. I asked him if he was going to Cambridge, to which he replied, "Yes and then on to Norwich." The penny then dropped! I said, "Are you going to the Number 2 I.T.C. at Britannia Barracks?" "Yes." We swapped names and it turned out that his Dad kept the Thornhill Arms at Rushton and his brother had a dance band. So we palled up together to join the Army. The date was 6 August 1942.

We arrived in Norwich at the Thorpe Station, which was the only one in use as the City station had been bombed very badly. Leaving the station we crossed the road and walked along the side of the River Wensum, where, looking to our left we could see the Cathedral through the trees. After a short time we turned right and walked up the very steep hill called Ketts which led us to the front and guardroom of Britannia Barracks, where we were all checked in and shown our sleeping quarters. Then we were paraded and taken to the stores to be given all our kit, clothes and a rifle, which you guarded with your life! The first night there we were shown the deep slit trenches all the way round the sleeping quarters and if the air-raid warning was sounded we would immediately get out of the building. When the German bombers came over the North Sea they had to cross over Great Yarmouth, so the Observer Corps rang through to Norwich, and we had what they called a crash call come through, which meant that we had about four minutes to get out of bed and into our trenches. Sure enough the second night that we were there the call came through, and into our trenches we jumped, with our tin hats on. The bombers came towards Norwich, and what we did not know was that the airport about half a mile away had an ack-ack battery which let fly with all its guns. Consequently we, in our open slit trenches, were more likely to be injured (with the theory that what goes up must come down) by the shrapnel, and this is what nearly happened. The other two I was sharing the trench with heard something smack into the ground near where they were crouching and felt in the dark for it. One of them let out a yell and said he had burnt his hand. He found out the hard way that shrapnel is still hot when it lands back on the ground. We were glad when the all clear sounded.

We had quite a few raids over a nine-week period and men from the barracks would help with the rescue of people from the rubble, with air-raid wardens, firemen and ambulance crews. One night those who went to help came back and said a bomb had landed on the Brewery and had split the large tanks that held the beer, and the street and the gutter were swamped with the beer which was disappearing down the drains. Some of the heavy drinkers never got over the shock!

I made friends with a Londoner whose surname was Hopkins, so his nickname was Hoppy! He was a good amateur boxer. One night we decided to go to a cinema in Norwich. When we were shown to our seats down the front there was this large area without any seats, and it had been concreted where they should have been. Turning to some people sitting nearby, we asked what had happened. The cinema had received a direct hit and people had been killed in that part. Hoppy and I decided that if the siren sounded we would leave straight away.

The sergeant who was in charge of us had to turn us out like fighting soldiers in six weeks – he never had a chance! When we were drilling and given a left turn, two thirds managed it and the rest turned right. And when it came to the last parade and the six weeks were up, two still got it wrong. We never had a weekend pass like the other platoons, we just had extra drills!

We finished with Britannia Barracks and moved down the hill to Nelson Barracks, which were the old horse barracks in the First World War. In the room where we were billeted the floors were still the old granite sets and drains.

During the months of November and December the barracks were a very cold place. It did, however, hot up one day. We were sitting around cleaning our rifles when one of our comrades shut the bolt to and pressed the trigger. The noise of the shot going off made us all dive different ways, with the bullet ricocheting off the old stone wall and granite floor till it was spent. How we escaped injury or death in that room, we shall never know! We were given a test to see what we were best suited for at Nelson Barracks. Some joined the Carrier platoon, Pioneer or Anti-tank platoon. I and three others joined the 3 inch Mortar and Sergeant Banthorpe was in charge of us. He turned out to be a gem. He taught us how to drive the carriers, mostly all around Norfolk to places like North Walsham, Aylsham, East Dereham, Wymondham, Great Yarmouth and once to Bungay in Suffolk. On one of these trips, driving along a quiet country lane (or so we thought), we were about to go round a bend, when out of nowhere there came this large American lorry with those large grills sticking out in the front, and over on our side of the road. It hit our carrier with such force that we went onto the verge, where a tree had been cut down leaving a stump about three foot across and about nine inches above the verge. We landed on this and could not move either way. Carriers are well built with quarter inch steel on the bottom and sides.

We were shook up but no blood was spilt and all we suffered was a dented mudguard. Climbing out we walked across to the truck, which had the entire front smashed in and the driver still in one piece. He started getting out, a bit dazed but recovering, saying that he would have to get the recovery vehicle out to tow him back to base. At that moment a farm tractor came along and the driver saw us stuck on the stump, had a good laugh and offered to pull us off, which he managed to do and get us back on to the road. He then told the GI where the nearest phone was. We left and carried on with our journey.

We trained with the 3 inch mortar with a crew of three. No.1 laid the sight on an aiming post, No.2 placed the bomb down the barrel (keeping his head away from the end of the barrel!), and No.3 prepared the bombs, and then we would all change position so that we could do any of the three positions.

The day dawned when we were to go to the firing range and fire live ammunition for the first time and as it turned out, nearly our last time! We drove to the range with our sergeant in our carrier with the mortar which was fixed in position on the back in three separate pieces. On arriving, our officer who would be in charge of the shoot, came on a motorcycle and parked it near our carrier.

We unloaded the mortar and were told where to set it up ready for firing and that it would be a short range shoot and the range would be anything from 100 yards to 500 yards. As I was No.3 it was my duty to prepare the bomb for that range, which would mean that the six packets of incendiaries, which propel the bomb from the barrel, had to be reduced to three, and the three that I had taken out were thrown onto the ground next to the bomb cases. We were firing smoke bombs and everything was going well, until some pieces of burning debris fell onto the packets that I had thrown on the ground. They burst into flames near my leg and made me jump back in shock to avoid being burnt.

Our sergeant saw what was happening and told us to take cover in some shallow ground, which I can tell you we did very quickly! The fire now spread to the bombs which if they got too hot would explode. The sergeant yelled to get into a ditch another forty yards further away. He had tried, with a fire extinguisher, to put out the fire, but to no avail. Then the motorcycle that was left nearby caught fire. He now took cover himself and he was just in time as one of the mortar bombs exploded, throwing phosphorus everywhere, which if it lands on your skin causes horrible burns. After a few more minutes most of them had finally blown up. When everything had quietened down, our sergeant came over to see if we were OK and said he did not know where the officer had gone!

Why did this accident happen, we asked our sergeant. Had we done anything wrong? He told us that as it was a short range shoot three of the incendiaries packets were lying around the ground. A very strong wind was blowing from left to right, the debris which comes out of the barrel when they are fired was burning and a small piece of this had dropped on to the heap around my legs – and up they went. This all happened in 1942 - by the time of D-Day, the range of the mortar had been extended and hardly any flammable pieces came out of the barrel.

We walked back to the carrier which was covered with phosphorous and started cleaning up the mess. It was now getting dark so we left and drove back to Nelson Barracks and parked the carrier inside the garage. The three of us stood there thinking what a lucky lot we were, having a sergeant who had looked after his men.

The outcome of this was that there had to be a court of inquiry about the incident, and that the three of us would be called to give evidence. We did see the officer again who told us we were not needed in court after all. I suspect he talked his way out of a court martial by blaming other people.

Christmas was approaching and I went to see the film in which Bing Crosby sang "White Christmas" and which I enjoyed as I had quite a few of his records.

One thing of note that happened one lunch time occurred when we had just washed our mess-tins and were walking back across the barrack square to our quarters. There were men everywhere, when a burst of firing made us look up and there above us at about three hundred feet was a Dornier, firing its guns. I have never seen so many men disappear in such a short space of time, and one man who was behind a door on the top balcony of our block was hit.

After Christmas men were being posted to different places like Sheringham where the Northants regiment were stationed. Into the New Year nothing had happened, when one day someone asked, "What are you doing here?" and asked my name. "Paine," I replied and had to follow him to the Company office. Looking through their list they said I should have gone to Sheringham, and then they found a Paine had already gone there. Apparently a policeman of the same name had been sent there.

The next day I went with a group of five others on a posting to Newquay, catching the train from Norwich and into Liverpool Street and then across to Paddington where we had a one hour wait. Finally we left at 10.00 pm on the Penzance train, with the six of us all in one compartment, two sleeping on the luggage racks and the rest of us spread all over the seats. We put a strap round the door handles just to ensure complete privacy! It was then boots off and get your head down.

Around 2 a.m. we stopped at another station and decided we had better open the door to let some fresh air in, and being next to the door I stood up and pushed it open to see that it was Bath. What I did not know was that someone's boot had fallen out onto the platform. Suddenly the guard came by and slammed the door to, then it was opened again by the guard holding an army boot in his hand saying that he nearly kicked it under the train and with that, he closed the door. Well we all had a good laugh saying we could just imagine someone getting out at Newquay station and being met by the R.S.M. and on parade standing there with one boot missing. Who lost it? Yes, it was mine! I broke out in a cold sweat thinking of the consequences.

We all finally went back to sleep again, while our journey in the early hours took us to Exeter, Plymouth and later on to a station called Par. Being near the door, I heard a shout just outside the coach, "Par station, change here for Newquay." It was sheer chance that I was awake with cramp in my leg that saved us from going on to Penzance! I yelled loud to wake them up and inform them that they had about two minutes to get out before the train left.

You have never seen such chaos that went on in those two minutes. Not one of us had any boots on, and our kit was all over the place and under the seats. Someone said, "Let's get it all on the platform and sort it out there." When the train departed, the people who looked out of the windows as they left saw us lot standing there bootless, with rifles, kit bags and gas masks lying about and must have thought that was Fred Karno's Army! We were lucky that the train which would take us on the last lap of our journey was already waiting on another platform.

We sorted ourselves out and boarded the coach and made good use of the time it took to Newquay to get properly dressed and look like soldiers. It was not too long before we crossed the viaduct over Trenance Gardens and into the station to wonder what awaited us. We opened the door, passed all our kit out onto the platform, not knowing what to do next, when this little man came marching towards us with a cane stuck under his arm. He turned out to be the Regimental Sergeant Major (known as the RSM) and he soon made sure that we knew it. We were made to line up while he inspected us, saying, "I will soon straighten you lot out!" I was glad that he had not seen us at Par Station.

He marched us out of the station and up to H.Q. which had been a hotel. (After the war my Mum and Dad stayed at this hotel and told me that there was a plaque on the wall saying that it was the H.Q. of the 70th Northants Regiment in 1942). He gave us orders as to which hotel we would be billeted in.

The six of us were split up, with me and another soldier going to the Tolcarne Hotel, which overlooked the beach of the same name. We were shown the room where we would sleep and it was a room on the third floor on the front with a wonderful view over the bay. To the left were the Harbour and Towan Head, below us the steps to the beach about eighty feet down to the sand, and to the right Lusty Glaze Beach. There was a NAAFI half-way down the footpath to Tolcarne Beach.

We were to stay for three months doing drill, rifle training on the cliff top called Barrowfields and cross country runs round the golf course and Fistral Beach, finishing in the sea on Tolcarne Beach. It was warm down here during that 1943 winter, with a few days of lovely sunshine, but mostly rain and drizzle.

But big changes were afoot. The 2nd Lincolns Regiment of the 3rd Infantry Division who were in France in 1940 under the charge of Monty were forced out by the German lightning advance, and were then taken off the Dunkirk beaches back to England. They were still short of men and were about to go to the Combined Training Centre at Inverary in Scotland.

After breakfast one morning, two hundred men went on parade and were told that they would be joining the 2nd Lincolns in the 3rd Division at Hythe, near Folkestone. Our Commanding Officer, Capt. Dominie, asked us to come to his office one at a time. As I went in he stood up and shook my hand, gave me twenty cigarettes and said, "Good luck, I hope you see it through." Thanking him, I saluted and left. During the next few months I always thought of those poignant words he had said.

We marched to the station, where a troop train stood ready to take us all the way to Hythe and the barracks at which we would be staying. The barracks also had a Martello Tower not far from where we would be doing guard duties. These duties were to patrol from a hotel on the sea front and report at the tower. Two of us were doing just that one dark night and were not far from the tower when a terrific explosion nearby made us lie flat on the ground with no idea what had happened. We plucked up courage and carried on to the guard room and asked what the big bang was. It was one of the big guns firing over to France.

When we were finally put into companies and platoons, I was placed in "D" Company and 16 Platoon and was put in charge of the 2 inch Mortar. The platoons moved around to different billets and it was our turn to move in. The hotel was on the sea front overlooking a small promenade, which had a dummy Bofor gun (light ack-ack) stationed just outside a window which had been blocked up.

We went to sleep that night and as the sun was rising we were woken by the noise of a plane travelling very fast and then firing what we thought were cannon shells into our part of the hotel. At the last moment it shot over the roof and returned back to France. Apparently the German fighters were leaving France as the sun was about to rise and skimming across the Channel at about twenty feet and by the time they reached the English coastline the sun was shining just above the sea making it hard for the gunners to see with the brightness straight into their eyes. Later on we had a walk round to the front of the hotel to see what the pilot had been firing at, and sure enough, he had given the dummy gun a good going over. We had now done a lot of training and route marches but it was nothing compared with what we would go through when we arrived at the Combined Ops in Inverary.

Chapter Two
Assault Training In Scotland

We travelled by troop train from Hythe Station round London and up the east coast line through Peterborough. I was looking out of the window when a Lincolnshire soldier who sat opposite said that he would be going by his house near a level crossing gate at Essendine and sure enough it flashed by before you were ready, and it would be another year before he had leave to go home. We carried on with our journey from Leeds across country to Carlisle, on to Glasgow, then past the Clyde and onto Crianlarich where we left the main line onto the branch line to Dalmally station. Here trucks would take us to our destination, to camps at the side of Loch Fyne and near to Inverary Castle. In this area we would have a varied schedule of training, with its arduous assault exercises and tough field firing schemes. The battalion was to be trained to a high degree of efficiency and physical fitness as the 3rd Division was destined to assault the beaches in Sicily.

Every kind of obstacle guarded most of the beaches all around Loch Fyne with barbed wire to make it hard work for the assault forces. Exercises included the din and the noise of artillery firing live ammunition and machine-gun fire. We returned to camp tired and dirty to be told that for political reasons our part in the Sicily landings would now be undertaken by the 1st Canadian Division.

In July 1943 we knew we were then destined to make a hole in Hitler's Atlantic Wall. Travelling from Inverary by truck to Dalmally and then by train north through Rannoch Moor and Spean Bridge where the Memorial to the Commandos stands, we arrived in the station at Fort William. After a time we moved northward through some lovely countryside by Loch Eil and pulled into a station called Glenfinnan. Here we left the train and piled in the trucks that stood waiting for us and proceeded along a road that hugged the loch on one side and a mountain on the other, wondering if we would arrive safely.

It was a long journey and we passed Beinn Resipol, and into the small village of Salen and from here we moved to the hamlet of Glenborrodale which would be our home for five or six weeks. The billets were the old Nissen huts – anyway they were better than tents!

They gave us a day to get over our journey and we were then thrown into the thick of it. We left in the morning to march in single file north across the Ardnamurchan peninsula - a distance of six miles to a little inlet called Kentra Bay. This was a very tiring exercise across lumps of heather and hollows where you could easily turn your ankle, damp and boggy ground, and we were very happy to arrive at our destination, where we had our haversack rations to fortify us for our next move onto a tough battle-course. We were only in denims, and had to take our rifles. We moved down onto a lovely sandy beach. With the hot sun beating down, we moved to a large outcrop of huge rock which climbed above our heads a hundred feet or more, and hanging down from the top was a rope ladder. Two sergeants were keeping an eye on us and giving the orders and told us to get climbing, but on the ladder to keep a gap of about six feet between each person. It all looked plain sailing, but as we climbed this shaking rope ladder it began to get harder as the rock face gradually began to move out of the perpendicular. The rope I must state was fixed to the rocks at yard intervals at this point of the climb, and we were pleased when we had finally passed this huge bulge on the rock face. How we all made it to the top without anyone falling off, we shall never know! At the top of this climb the ground levelled out and the two sergeants showed us the next obstacle that our platoon had to cross. We walked to the edge of a ravine which had a drop of twenty or thirty feet, with a tree trunk laid over the gap which we had to cross.   The thickness of the tree was about one foot. "Nothing to it", the sergeant said. "Only one fell in it with the previous platoon!" We were the second platoon and as we took a closer look at the log we realised that it was wet and muddy and wished we were somewhere else! "Right, get weaving," said our corporal. One of our comrades set off on this twenty foot journey slipping once or twice, regaining his balance and made it. Most of us made it, but one slipped and straddled the log, which I guess hurt a bit? He finally made it sitting on his backside.

After that stunt there could not be anything worse than that! But there was a sardonic smile on the sergeant's face. We followed them across some tracks climbing higher, when they suddenly stopped at the edge of a very long drop. Going up to the edge myself and peering over, it looked like a forty foot drop. I drew back quickly before I fell over, thinking that this would be the end of an Army career!

I then had another look and saw something that I had missed - a fir tree, with all the branches cut off. The sergeants had now joined us and with delight told us what to do. You stand as close to the edge as you can get, and grab the tree with both arms and at the same time your legs will lock round and then slide to the bottom! The first one to try was a small chap, so when he leaned out to catch hold of it – guess what – yes, it was just out of his reach. The sergeant gave a smile and said, "Well bloody well jump then." Which he did and got a reasonable grip with his arms and legs, but the platoon who were in front of us had left a certain amount of mud about on the trunk of the tree, and his journey down the tree was quicker than he intended. When he arrived at the bottom his hands were very sore and it didn't do his ankles a lot of good. I was next and being six foot with long arms, when I leaned over I could get my hands on the tree, and the fear of seeing what happened to the other soldier spurred me on to give an almighty jump. I grasped the tree with arms and legs and went down to land with a jolt, very glad to have made it, as most of the platoon did. We had a bit of a break at this stage and tucked into our haversack rations. After the rest we were taken to some higher ground where we were told to keep running all the time and not to stop. Halfway down we would come to some logs placed across the track which we must jump without putting our feet on them (like a horse jumping a hurdle). If the officer watching caught you using your feet, he would send you back to do it again! We were doing all this with our rifles slung across our backs which we were supposed to keep clean at all times (some hope!).

We started going down the hill with boulders and loose scree about, and when I arrived at the logs and seeing no officer about, I stepped on the logs and jumped and cleared the deep mud and water on the other side. I started running down the course, when a voice rang out near a tree. Yes, it was the officer, yelling at me to "go back and do it again - and jump the logs this time." I went back to the top of the hill again thinking what a silly idiot I had been.

I started back down the hill again and as I jumped to clear the logs I caught the top log, and went over head-first down about five feet, legs flying, my rifle banging my shoulder, into about four feet of mud and water, and crawled out feeling sorry for myself. One of the sergeants came up to me and said, "I told you to keep that rifle clean." "Yes Sarge."

For the next exercise the platoon came right down off the hills to a fast-flowing river where we were all handed a toggle rope which we hung round our shoulders. Near where we were all standing was a very tall fir tree with branches cut off but leaving nine inches, which would help us climb about forty feet near to the top. Here a thick rope was tied firmly round the trunk and sloped away over the river to the iron pole on the river bank.

One of our sergeants was at the top of the tree to ensure we put our toggle ropes on correctly and over the rope, which we would slide down. Checking everything for safety he gave me a quick push and away I went across the river to land on the river bank. After we had all got across, the officer said that when the Canadians had done the same thing, one of their soldiers had fallen off into the river, which was very fast flowing, and was drowned, and it took four days before they found his body! We were glad they did not tell us before.

After the end of that exercise we marched back the way we had come, and arrived back at our camp very tired and weary men. The next day dawned bright and sunny and after parade we were told we would be climbing a mountain called Beinn Resipol which was 2772 feet high and we would be taken up by a Lord Lovat Scout. We were taken in trucks along the coast road, through Salen for about a mile where we stopped at the place where we would begin our climb. It was a gradual climb at the start and after half a mile it really began to get very steep. Our company of about a hundred and fifty men followed the scout in single file over a narrow footpath with a huge drop each side. When we started the climb we had our pullovers tied round our waists ready to use when we got cold, the higher we climbed. We were all sweating profusely when the scout passed back the word to put them on. We must have been fit men to keep up the pace, but we were glad when we made it to the top. We were very lucky that the weather was clear and bright and I have never seen such a view before. I could see all of the Ardnamurchan Peninsula and the Outer Hebrides in the far distance and to my left not far away was the Island of Mull. Turning right round I could see Fort William in the distance, and Ben Nevis rising to its 4409 feet. I can only say that I felt on top of the world.

Suddenly we were told by a sergeant that the record for getting off this mountain slope to the main road was eight minutes timed to when the last man was in the trucks. The sergeant yelled, "Go! Go!" and off we went. There were rocks small and large in the way, but down we ran trying to keep our balance. We were gaining momentum all the time but could not do anything about it. Some fell and recovered, and we all made it to the road, but with aching limbs and sore ankles we scrambled into the backs of the lorries. I forget whether we beat the record.

We were very weary men going back to camp, and glad that we had transport. Arriving back we were told that in two days' time we would be carrying out a landing on the Island of Rhum. We had the next day to clean our rifles and equipment, and have a good rest ready for the following day.

The day of the landing was dry and sunny, and we hoped it would stay that way for our sea crossing. The boats we would be using held about twenty-five men and were driven by a diesel engine. I think they were called 'cobble boats.'

We gathered on the quayside at around 8pm and a nice evening looked in prospect, so I walked across to one of the old fishermen and said, "It looks set fair for tonight." He grunted and had a look at the sky, and then said it would be blowing hard by midnight. It took me back a bit and I hoped he was wrong. I think it was a Navy man in charge at the helm, and by the end of the night he turned out to be very good at his job. We sailed out of Loch Sunart passing the lighthouse on Ardnamurchan Point and then later on the islands of Muck and Eigg. By midnight the wind was whipping up the sea, and making life unpleasant. Added to that the smell of the diesel fumes made those that sat near to it feel a bit queasy. At around two or three in the morning we had to get in the lee of the headquarter vessel until the wind decreased. We moved nearer to Rhum and the north headland of Rubha Shamhnan, and with the dawn beginning to break the boats began moving in towards the beach and we were told to get our equipment ready. I put my rifle around my shoulder and the 2 inch Mortar that I carried around my neck, as that was the best way to carry it, with the barrel and base plate in the shape of the letter V. "Prepare to land," we were told by the sailor as he cut the engine, and then "Go! Go!" We had no proper landing craft at this time so we had to jump over the side which was about five foot above the sea. I thought I would get it over with quickly before the sea got a little crowded, and over I went. In the next few seconds I hit the water and went down and down, and the coldness of it, and I hoped I could stand on the bottom and was glad when I did, with the water up to my chest. Others were jumping in now and one or two who were on the small side had difficulty keeping their heads above water. We started moving towards the beach which we could see a little more clearly now that the sun was getting higher in the sky. The beach was still two hundred yards away, when someone shouted, "It's getting deeper," and those who could not swim – including me – were getting in a bit of a panic. What happened was that we had hit a sand bank, and we were lucky that the water had only been three or four feet deep!

Anyway, as we moved nearer to the beach we were greeted with machine gun fire, firing on fixed lines just over our heads, to get us used to being under fire. We finally made it to the beach and moved south past

Kilmory and two mountains on either side of us which were around nine hundred feet high and shrouded in mist and rain. We marched through to Kinloch Castle, where we were allowed to take shelter in some outbuildings in the castle grounds. We had a brew up and tried to dry our clothes, and we then tried to get some sleep before the boats picked us up in the morning. We had just about nodded off when it started to rain heavily and we were all getting wet again. I then realised that there were a lot of slates missing off the roof! We were glad to get on the boats the next morning and return to Glenborrodale after an exercise that had been carried out in such bad weather conditions. This was an experience never to be forgotten.

A far more unpleasant period in combined operations was to be in store for us, with an approach to what D-Day would be like. We sailed back through the Sound of Mull to Oban, where a train would take us to Dalmally and south through some lovely scenery by Loch Long, past Helensburgh and into Glasgow and then along the southern banks of the Clyde to Greenock. Here we loaded onto one of the old paddle steamers which would take us past Rothesay on the Isle of Bute and then through the Kyles of Bute to a place called Tighnabruaich. The camp here was under canvas, pitched on the side of a hill, and with rain and high winds the living conditions were intolerable. With ten men to a Bell tent and beds damp and muddy, tempers did flare up at times and to crown it all the mess-tent blew down one night in a force eight gale. Under a damp and cloudy sky in September in the area of Kilbride Bay, which was the name of the exercise, we landed in the bay and found ourselves wading two hundred yards to get ashore!

The following day on the next exercise called Millhouse, after we had done some training lying on the ground taking cover, we saw what our artillery could do in support, and also the accuracy of our anti-tank guns. This was followed by the Lincolns infantry working with the Churchill tanks which moved up behind us and started firing the guns and their Besa machine guns just above our heads.

After this intensive training, we were told that this was the wettest place in Scotland (and I agree that's right) and we were glad when we embarked to sail to Greenock. Here we boarded a troop train to take us to an area between Beauly and Dingwall near Inverness.

Our journey north from Greenock took us through Glasgow, Falkirk and Stirling, passing near to where the Battle of Bannockburn took place in 1314. We were now going through some beautiful scenery of mountains and moors, lochs and glens, past Perth and on to Pitlochry where the mountains reach over 3000 feet or more. This journey by train right through the heart of the Highlands gave me immense pleasure to see the beauty of Scotland in all its glory of sun, rain and then snow! We had now passed through Inverness and were running alongside Beauly Firth, and at the end we pulled in to Beauly station where we were glad to stretch our legs. We were then taken by lorries to a camp, again in tents, with the New Year nearly upon us.

The reason we had travelled all this way was that this part of Scotland east of Inverness had been selected as the nearest to the coastline in France chosen for our assault in the year to come. This exercise was for the 9th British Infantry Brigade to practise its role of reserve brigade to pass through the assaulting brigades and capture and hold ground of importance.

The beaches we landed on were Culbin Sands and Burghead Bay. One of the landings was named Grab in December 1943 and the other named Leap Year in March 1944. On Grab we landed in four feet of water in a blizzard, and 16 platoon of D Company, which I was in at the time, had to climb up to some high ground to a forest with our clothes still wet and water in our boots. Darkness was approaching and we were told to dig slit trenches as the enemy was nearby, but the ground was so frozen that we made little impression. We had umpires dashing here and there saying that a shell had landed among two or three men and they were dead. We knew from how cold it was getting around midnight that we would soon be dead. We spoke to our corporal about making a fire behind a stone built wall and he agreed with us. We found paper in our packs like old letters and newspapers and we finally had a fire going using broken branches off the trees. To feel the heat of the fire was a lovely feeling and our clothes were beginning to dry out. In the distance someone yelled "Put that fire out!" One of our lot yelled "Not on your Nellie!!"

After a short time on the hillside some more fires were being started, and most of us firmly believed that without them we would have struggled to make it through the night with the temperature well below zero and the chill wind in December. We found out in the morning that they had decided to let the men dry themselves out and keep warm if they could on that very cold hillside. After this exercise had finished we were billeted in a little town called Keith. Our quarters were in an old brewery and after living under canvas in the Beauly area it was luxury indeed. When we were at Beauly they laid on a three ton truck to take us into Dingwall, so with a couple of mates off we went. On arriving there we decided to go straight to a café and have a fish and chip meal with a double helping of chips! Feeling rather full and satisfied we found the only cinema, which was showing the film called "Casablanca," which I enjoyed. The song "As Time Goes By" was a reminder that our time was going by when we had to get a foothold on the Continent of Europe.

We finally moved from the north of Scotland and were in an area around Selkirk, St. Boswells and Galashiels. D Company moved into a large house called Broadmeadow. We learnt how to lie on our stomachs in the cold wet fields at ten o'clock at night, prodding for dummy mines with our bayonets. Sometimes we had a run and walk march to keep us fit, where we would run a mile and walk the same distance with all our equipment.

The next move was south to Stobs Camp about two miles from Hawick. The camp, we were told, was a First World War camp for P.O.Ws. It was in Hawick that the Lincolns were given the freedom of the town and were allowed to march through the streets.

One afternoon at Stobs Camp I decided to "get my head down" until tea time, when most of the men had gone into Hawick for the afternoon. When walking back to my hut from the wash-house, a shout rang out across the square calling me over to where a truck stood with men getting on board. It turned out to be an officer who asked me to make up the rugby team because they were one short. I quickly replied, "I know nothing about rugby and anyway I haven't any boots." He turned to one of the sergeants, "Get some boots," and shoved me straight into the back of the lorry where I joined the rest of the team. Two or three pairs of boots were thrown in for me to try on. I felt completely bewildered and I could not do a lot about it. The journey took us to Hawick Rugby Ground where a river ran along one side of the pitch. In the pavilion I was given a shirt and shorts and found a pair of boots that I could move my toes in. The officer took me to one side and said, "Look, you're about six feet tall. When we get a lineout you just knock the ball back and we will do the rest. OK?" I nodded my head but not with much conviction. When I came down the steps the opposition were already kicking the ball about and were all over six feet and sixteen stone! I asked who they were, and one of the sergeants said, "It's the "Paddies" (Royal Ulster Rifles) who were in the 9th Brigade. The whistle blew and the ball was kicked off. I followed behind feeling a right prat! After a few minutes we had a lineout, and someone pushed me into it. The ball came over and picked me out. I half-heartedly threw my hand at it, and to my disbelief I knocked it back to one on our side, who all then rushed away from me and scored a try. The officer came back to me and said, "Good show - keep it up." Half time came and we had a drink. The R.U.R. kicked off this time and the ball finished in the river, which was fast flowing but only two feet deep and you had to hope you caught the ball before it disappeared from sight round a bend in the river!

The game carried on and I was just getting the hang of it, when the inevitable happened – someone passed the ball to me! So I thought I had better run with it, to show willing, going towards the opposition, when these two huge Irishmen confronted me. In my panic I threw the ball away, I know not where! There was a lot of running and shouting and the Lincolns had scored again. The officer came running back saying, "A brilliant pass!" patting me on the back. Little did he know I was glad to get shot of the ball. The game finished and we arrived back at Stobs Camp. The officer came over to me and said, "Can you play next week?" The following week I went out early with the lads and kept well away from the square where the lorry was parked!

One Sunday night my pal and I came on the bus from Broadmeadows to go to the cinema in Selkirk, and when we arrived we had already seen the film. We walked a bit aimlessly along the main street wondering what to do. Drinking in a pub did not appeal to us, and when a lady of middle age spoke to us saying that we looked lost, we told her what had happened.

She said would we like to come to her house and she would cook a supper for us. We said we would enjoy having a meal at her home. It was only a street away to her house, where she showed us into her front room and told us to make ourselves at home. She certainly kept her house spick and span, and in a little while she asked us to come through to her small dining room, where on the table were two lovely cooked meals and mugs of tea. I noticed on the dresser a photograph of a young man in Navy uniform, and I asked if it was her son, and what ship was he serving on. She turned to me and said with tears in her eyes that his ship had been sunk in the Atlantic! What could I say to comfort her? I was only a young soldier of twenty years old who had never suffered the death of someone close, like her young son whom she would never see again.

However, she quickly gained her composure and cleared away the plates and came back to talk to us again saying that if we came again to Selkirk and wanted to use her bathroom, she would provide the hot water, which we thought was very kind of her (but we would need to bring the soap – it was very scarce). Apparently we were not the only ones that she had helped - anyone in the forces she would talk to and offer a meal or cup of tea. She told us that having no son of her own now, it was the only way she could help the war effort and that when her son was alive, people had done the same for him in England and other places.

Saying goodbye to this caring person, we thanked her very much as we ran to catch the bus back to Broadmeadows. Sadly we never met again. In the middle of April 1944 we said farewell to the Border country which we knew so well to travel south as far as we could go, to Portsmouth.

Chapter Three
Final Preparations, D-Day and Caen

We were in Camp A12, a tented camp in Creech Wood near the village of Denmead which was only two or three miles from the place where the first cricket club, Hambledon Cricket Club, was formed in 1750. Also in this area King George VI inspected the troops of the 3rd Infantry Division. This was the final stage, getting ready for the big "D". One of our last exercises was called Fabius 4. Naval Assault Forces landed the 3rd Division between Littlehampton and Bognor Regis to test the inter-service operation.

The mortar platoon, which I had since joined from 16 platoon in D Company, was transported mostly by carriers and it saved a lot of wear and tear on your boots. Being in a company you carried everything on your back, so it was a luxury to be mobile on a vehicle. I was sorry to say goodbye to my mates in D Company, and as we went our separate ways we were conscious that we might not meet again.

After landing near to Littlehampton, we passed Monty standing in his jeep giving us a wave as we drove by. We moved inland and took the carriers into a field. Just two carriers remained and the rest went elsewhere. We set the mortars up behind a barn wall and prepared bombs for firing (this was all pretend, with officers in white coats who were umpires). We then had a brew up while we awaited further orders. After two hours most of us had dropped off to sleep when suddenly we heard a motorbike coming nearer to us, and into the field came an umpire on a B.S.A. bike.

He set the motorbike up on its stand and walked slowly towards us. "Who's in charge here?" We pointed to the sergeant who had been asleep around the side of the carrier, and was hardly awake, saying, "What's all the noise about?" But when he saw the officer he quickly saluted, shouting out,

"Sir." The officer looked at our slovenly appearance and said a large shell had landed just where we were standing and we were all dead. With that he mounted his motorcycle and departed out of sight. I wondered what would happen now and whether we would be put on a charge, but it was not to be. The sergeant said that the operation was due to finish the next day, so we could get the tarpaulins off the back of the carriers, and tie them onto the vehicle to form a roof like a bivouac. Two or three of us walked to the pub in a nearby village, some wrote letters, one made a brew up, and I read a book. It was a hot sunny day. Later on they decided to find a chip shop. We had taken one of the tarpaulins off the end of the carrier, and off they went on a "recce!" When they had enough money from a whip round, they came back with some delightful fish and chips. The day passed quickly and we soon made ourselves comfortable and had a good night's sleep under the stars. The next day we packed the carriers with the mortars on the back and were on the road to Lyminster and through to Arundel. We went up the steep hill to the castle, round the sharp turn in the road at the top and onto Chichester and the harbour, turning off the main road to Waterlooville and Denmead to our camp in Creech Wood.

We now spent time waterproofing our carriers and also checking our equipment before we were sealed in the camp. The mortar platoon visited a range on the South Downs behind Worthing, where the bombs were given better secondary charges and new sights were needed for the longer range which had never been achieved before. Our commanding officer was Lt. J. C. Roll, and in our section I teamed up with number 1, Johnny Goodson from Gedney Dyke, number 2 I think was Chippy, and number 3 was yours truly who prepared the bombs for firing. When you think that we kept the same crew right through to the end, you can appreciate how lucky we were. Our driver however was not so lucky. He was killed by a direct hit on his slit trench when a German 88 gun fired around twenty shells.

Getting back to the story, when we arrived back at camp, barbed wire was erected around the camp and we were finally sealed in and guarded. No one was allowed out at all! From then on we had no contact with the world outside. During the first week in June the senior officers "who were in the know" spent most of their time in the operations room at Brigade HQ preparing to brief the battalion for the biggest battle that it had ever had the privilege and honour to participate in. This briefing took place on the 29th May, and the next day we were split up into landing craft loads and into camps to await "sailing orders."

On the morning of 5th June we moved down to Southsea Pier with S Company, where they started to load the vehicles onto the L.C.Ts. I had been warned that I would have to travel with the Royal Ulster Rifles on their landing craft, as I was one body too many for the Lincoln's landing craft.

We lay at anchor for a time. I made myself known to the sergeant of the anti-tank gun and gained permission to ride off on their carrier when we arrived in France.

The skipper said that if we weighed anchor at 1800 hours we should know it was "on". And sure enough we did and with the issue of maps now seen for the first time by most people, we knew then that the invasion of Europe was a reality. I had a look around the L.C.T. and decided the best spot was a small compartment where they lowered the ramp to let the vehicles off. I put my rifle kit inside, and had a walk around the landing craft until it began to get dark. Saying goodnight to the lads I would leave with in the morning, I made myself as comfortable as possible in my very small compartment. I lay there wondering what tomorrow held for us, but I was very tired and it had been a busy day. As dusk fell I was soon asleep.

Little did I realise what I would wake up to in the morning but we had been told that the R.A.F. had promised that not one hostile aircraft would be allowed to attack our convoy, and the Navy would land us safely and in the right place. We had confidence in ourselves to carry out the plan we knew so well.

I awoke to the movement of the boat and the sounds of planes overhead and firing on the beach in front. We were standing well offshore as the Lincolns were to follow up after the South Lancs and East Yorks had made the initial landing. I think we started moving into the beach around 1 pm and as we got closer, I could see over the side of the L.C.T. about four feet away a stake in the sand with a large teller-mine attached to it. We were now getting very close to the beach and the tanks and carriers started warming up their engines, ready for the drive off.

It was at this time that I found out what being in action meant as someone was making our landing very difficult with accurate fire from the shore. I collected my rifle and kit and clambered aboard the anti-tank gun I was to ride upon, just as the L.T.C. grounded on the beach. The ramp was dropped very quickly and everyone tried to get away and off the beach as quickly as they could.

We arrived on the beach OK – I suppose you could call it a dry landing - and began to move towards the exit when a vehicle in front hit a mine and blocked the way between the white tapes. The sergeant of the Royal Ulster

Rifles yelled to unhook the gun, so I jumped down to help the other men pull the gun out of the way, while the carrier backed out of the exit. Despite the soft sand and some German shells landing nearby we soon had the job done and jumped aboard to leave by another exit two hundred yards away. However as we approached, several shells landed very close, so the sergeant decided to go back to the first exit. By now a tank had cleared a way through, so we finally made our way along the track and joined the road to Hermanville-sur-Mer. There I parted from the lads of the Royal Ulster Rifles and started walking towards the village, looking into orchards to try and find my mates.

There were still a few shells about and distant machine gun fire and I began to wonder if I would find my platoon when I heard a shout. "Come on, we're over here." I moved very quickly and joined them, only to be asked, "What kept you?" I then followed them into the field where the mortar platoon were digging deep pits to set the mortars in. I was greeted by my No.1 Johnny Goodson with a spade and the command "Get digging," which I did with Chippy, the No.2. After all that Lt. Roll came along and ordered us to dig our slit trench, so that we could stand to at dusk. Whilst digging the slit trench we had got about eighteen inches down when a German plane came over dropping some butterfly bombs. Both of us dived in the same trench with me in last – my backside felt very exposed! We were lucky that the bombs fell in a nearby field.

Sometime later we were ordered by the sergeant to stand to in our mortar pits with rifles at the ready as a German attack with Tiger tanks was expected. This gave our stomachs a nasty turn, but we learnt later that after a lot of heavy firing they had moved round us.

On the second day we fired a lot of smoke for the Infantry Company to attack the château and village of Lion-sur-Mer. The château was a strong point and held the attack off. One or two hours later the battalion was sent to the village of St Aubin d'Arquenay, where we took up a defensive position guarding the bridge at Bénouville, which the 6th Airborne had captured in the morning.

I still have in my possession two postcards that lay in the rubble of a damaged house near the road – one of the village and the other of Caen before we bombed it. We were only in the spot for one day and I shall never forget the jeeps coming back to the beaches bearing stretchers with the wounded and dying airborne soldiers in an endless stream. I felt very sad to see such good soldiers taking so much punishment.

On the third day after a hectic night we moved back over the river to Cambes. We set the mortars up behind a wood, digging pits so that they could clear the trees. On the first morning there in the early hours all was quiet so I had returned to my slit trench to fetch something, when I heard a plane about three hundred yards away, very low. It was machine-gunning the carriers parked alongside the woods. I must say I made the last thirty yards in world record time. After the plane had gone, it left three or four fires burning, as it had hit the jerry cans on the back of the carriers. All in all we counted ourselves lucky.

We stayed quite a while in the Cambes wood and Galmanche area and during this time storms in the Channel played havoc with our supplies. As a result we could only fire the mortars if the Infantry Company needed help. We remained in the area until the end of June, sometimes changing positions along a sunken road. Every day at midday we were shelled for around fifteen minutes. We even dug out pits so that we could put the carriers below ground level. Nevertheless we took a lot of casualties at that time.

Around the beginning of July this static period came to an end and the 9th Infantry Brigade moved back to the Orne River in the Bénouville - Blainville area in preparation for the attack on Caen. On the day before the attack the carrier and mortar group moved to a wood near to the Château Beauregard. The mortar platoon carried the mortars all the way to the new site where we dug some deep pits, which were to save our section's lives later on the next day. As we moved to this position we passed some infantry men digging slit trenches. Someone shouted to me "Hello Desborough!" and I looked across to see two men from my home town. We wished each other good luck and went our separate ways. Sadly one was later killed and the other one wounded.

During the evening of the 7th July we watched as the R.A.F. bombed the northern outskirts of Caen, followed by an attack on the Le Bisey area involving H.M.S. Rodney's 16 inch guns. The infantry moved forward and good initial progress was made by both the Royal Ulster Rifles and the Kings Own Scottish Borderers. However, when the 2nd Lincolns moved forward they met with stiff opposition and took many casualties. This was chiefly due to the German position in the factory at Colombelles, whose tall chimneys provided a perfect observation post. The mortar platoon was called to give a lot of supporting fire and smoke, so there was plenty to do.

After a while we were having a smoke when Captain Roll came to see if we were all OK. At that moment we heard in the distance a "Moaning

Minnie" fire and knowing that you had seven seconds to get your head down I said to the Captain that he should get into our pit. He refused, saying that he had to go and see the other mortars, and turned away. I threw myself into the pit, landing on Johnny Goodson in the process, just before the explosion roared around us. The soil that we had dug out filled our ears and eyes, and the air in our lungs seemed to be sucked out of us. My head was full of ringing bells. I cannot say how long we lay there or even whether we blacked out. We slowly sorted ourselves out and heard the cry "Stretcher bearers." We stood up and looked around, climbing out of the mortar pit to see Captain Roll lying several yards away. The stretcher bearers took him away to the R.A. post. They said later that there wasn't a mark on him – the bomb had landed at his feet and the blast had killed him. The bomb had landed in the soil that we had thrown out when we dug the pit, about three feet from the edge.

This battle cost the battalion dear with thirty-two killed, and six officers and a hundred and thirty-two other ranks wounded. We were relieved at the start of the second week in July and went back to the rest area near Lion-sur-Mer, less than half a mile from the beach where we had originally landed five weeks before.

During the stay at Luc-sur-Mer we serviced the carriers and also had to stock up with some 3 inch mortar bombs from the Royal Army Service Corps about twenty miles away. I was ordered to go with a driver and a 30 cwt truck and pick them up. When we found the place I contacted a sergeant who showed us where they were stacked and he checked them while we loaded the truck. Chatting to the sergeant at the time I asked if he happened to know of a John Paine in the RASC. He called out to the office tent, "John you're wanted," and there was my cousin John. We were both taken aback to have met in Normandy like that.

As we drove back to Luc-sur-Mer the fields on both sides of the road were filled with ammunition and "compo" rations – all the things to keep us going. We had one ration pack per carrier, which was for five men for one week. We also had a bag of Burton's biscuits (hard tack), and they certainly were. The packs were all letter stamped, A-B-C-D-E with all sorts of variations of tinned bully beef, bacon, baked beans etc. If you were lucky enough to get an "E" pack you got the extra luxury of tinned peaches. We later found out that these were hospital packs.

When we arrived back at the rest area, the sergeant called the platoon together and announced that we had bread. We all cheered, and then he gave us the punch line – only one loaf. That would have given us one very thin slice each, so with much moaning and groaning we agreed to cut cards for the loaf. I can't remember who won, but I know we were still on hard biscuits.

Our rest period near the coast was now coming to an end and we were preparing to go back into the thick of the battle, which had been going on around the Caen area. We moved east of the Orne River and concentrated in the area of Amfreville. We knew then that a big push to break the German defensive line was on.

Dawn broke on the 16th July as we stood to in the mortar pits and watched in awe as the R.A.F. swooped over us and bombed the German positions in the villages on the Sannerville plain. The ground shook from the explosions of the 4000 lb bombs, including fragmentation bombs, and seemed to go on for a long time. At last the bombers departed and the artillery put down a heavy barrage. At that moment we all wondered how anyone could live through all that. We could hear the movement of tanks and half-tracks nearby moving forward in this unearthly noise. Johnny Goodson, the "old solider" in our platoon, having been in the Lincolns in 1940, said that he would be glad when we did make a move out of the valley, as the mosquitoes from the River Dives had made his life miserable for the last two days. News came through of quick successes at Cuverville, Giberville, Démouville, Touffréville and Sannerville which were all entered in quick succession. At midday we finally received the order to move forward. At last the enemy were on the run.

However we were soon to discover that in the first flush of success we had underrated the enemy and forgotten his ability to hit back. They fell back, but only to a strongly prepared line, and when our armour moved forward, they found their way barred by powerful anti-tank guns. The Germans had no intention of giving ground in the area around Troarn, which was to be held until the last possible moment.

The 2nd Lincolns moved off into the devastated area of Sannerville under heavy shell fire. The mortar platoon dug in amongst the trees of an orchard well away from the rest of the company. We were never very popular anyway as we always attracted German mortar counter-fire. After digging the mortars in we had to dig a two-man slit trench and get a brew on and something to eat. At this time the Germans were using a lot of artillery and multi-rocket launchers, known as "moaning minnies". These were mostly blast bombs. After a few hours we had orders to move forward, so we reloaded the carriers and moved along a track by a wood. Suddenly we came to a halt as an infantryman called to the leading carrier that the enemy were just round the bend and firing at anyone who dared show their face. The sergeant therefore decided to return to our original mortar pit position.

During the operation to create a diversion towards the Caen to Troarn major road the battalion were based in this small area of orchard country which became known as "Black Orchard" as a result of the high number of casualties received. In all we lost ten officers including the Commanding Officer, eighteen other ranks, and one hundred and eighty-two other ranks wounded. At the same time the 1st K.O.S.B.and the 2nd R.U.R. were also suffering and making little headway advancing towards Troarn.

During our platoon's return from the wood to our original mortar position, we came under very heavy fire from a co-ordinated mortar and artillery defensive system. It was very frightening and all around seemed to be mayhem. The driver of our carrier, whose nickname was "Robbo" was told by our No.1, Johnny Goodson, to make for a nearby barn. Lucky for us it was open on one side, so we could drive straight in. The German fire was still very heavy all around so we all dived under the carrier, which seemed to be the safest place to be. Lying next to Johnny Goodson I remember shouting to him, "What about the bombs and petrol (two twenty-gallon tanks) above us?" I'll never forget his reply. "If we get one up there, our worries will all be over." We must have been in this position for over an hour when the firing gradually decreased and we decided to get back to our original position to set the mortars and to be ready to give fire if needed. As we drove back men were already being brought back to the First Aid post on jeeps and carriers.

We arrived back at our orchard to see some of the platoon already getting their mortars in position. On getting back to our original place we found that in our absence a shell had landed in the pit itself. Sitting with a brew after getting the mortar ready we thought how lucky we had been. Then the rains came, accompanied by thunder, turning the hard ground into soft Normandy clay. The Commanding Officer, Lt Col. Welby-Everard was hit by fragments of a mortar bomb whilst sheltering in a trench that received an almost direct hit. Major D.R. Wilson rejoined us and took command.

On the following day, 20th July, the battalion received the order to advance and re-occupy the ground from which it had been forced to withdraw the previous night. The mortar platoon was now moved to another position ready for the second attack. We dug the mortars in again in an area where the big bomb holes testified to the fact that the R.A.F. had done a good job.

I decided to dig my slit trench about half way down this thirty foot hole. I made a reasonable trench and was quite chuffed with it when suddenly all hell was let loose in our bit of orchard by a German "88". In the next two or three minutes about twenty shells landed in our area. I had just finished digging when the first shell landed so I threw myself into the hole and hoped for the best. While the ground above took a dreadful pounding, one shell landed in the crater on the other side and the explosion brought some of the soil down on my head, making it ring while my body shook. In the stillness after the shelling I lay a little while trying to collect my thoughts, when I heard calls all around for stretcher bearers. Clambering out of the crater, I was met by a scene of devastation. Two of the mortars had been damaged in their pits, slit trenches had taken direct hits and carriers had suffered badly. Helping and doing what we could we realised that the platoon had been devastated. Many men had been killed or injured. We helped one of the injured, our driver Robbo, to the First Aid Post. Our unit was now completely non-effective, with not a single senior N.C.O. remaining.

Around the 22nd July the battalion was relieved by the 1st South Lancashires and we moved to Escoville. In the two and a half days there we received about sixty reinforcements, including Capt. W.J. Parsons of the South Wales Borderers, who took command of our mortar platoon. I was sent to HQ Company to fetch the reinforcements for the mortar platoon. One of these men was Charlie Smith from the King's Regiment. Talking together we found that we had much in common and became very good friends, this friendship helping both of us to get through the war. Despite being still under strength (during the period we were in the orchard we were nineteen officers and nearly four hundred other ranks below complement) we left Escoville on the 25th July to relieve the 2nd Battalion East Yorks in the brickwork area north-west of Troarn. We spent a comparatively uneventful week there apart from the fact that I received a parcel. To my surprise it contained a cake made by my mother and a letter congratulating me on my coming of age, my twenty-first birthday being on the 28th July. I quickly had the cake out of the tin and shared it with Johnny and the rest of the crew. It tasted beautiful. I think I came of age a bit before my birthday.

Around the beginning of August we were relieved by our own 4th Battalion, our first contact with them in France. We then moved back again over the River Orne to the area around Biéville. We were expecting a week's rest but this was not to be. Following the American breakthrough from Avranches in the west, more infantry were now required in the vital Vire sector. So our 3rd British Infantry Division was moved by motor transport to the extreme right of the British 2nd Army front. It would be a long time before we were to operate as a Division again.

Chapter Four
Night Assault Crossing
of the Escaut Canal

We moved from Biéville and travelled west along the roads and tracks of Normandy to the Bocage country south of Bayeux where we spent a few nights in the peaceful surroundings of the St Martin des Besaces area. By this time we had received a hundred reinforcements and two full platoons from the 7th Battalion East Yorks.

We moved south towards Vire on the 6th August, aiming to cross a tributary of the River Vire by the main road at the Pont de Vaudrey. This bridge was covered by a strong enemy force in the village of Montisanger. The ground rose beyond the river towards the main road running due east from Vire, equally vital to the advancing Americans and to the Germans in retreat.

We were positioned in this area in a large field behind a small wood, following our usual procedure of digging in the mortars first, followed by a good brew on the cooker and a "nosh-up", when we suddenly realised that we had company at the far end of the field. Four or five men started walking towards us and it soon became obvious that they were G.Is. They were in a pretty friendly mood, greeting us with a "Hi, there, have a drink, buddy." It turned out that they had been in England only two weeks previously and, knowing that they were to be sent to Normandy, had spent two nights in London "on the town." They had also loaded themselves up with a lot of the "bottled stuff", which was now unfortunately nearly at an end.

We sat with them round our mortar pits, helping them to finish their few remaining bottles. We offered them some of our brew in return, which came as a surprise to them as it was rather on the strong side – you could probably have stood the spoon up in it. One of them was from Brooklyn and was a big Dodgers fan. Another one, who had a real Texan drawl, asked Johnny Goodson about a gun of ours he had heard being fired. He said it made a moaning sound, like something being wound up. We were puzzled until the penny dropped – he was describing the German's Nebelwerfer, or "Moaning Minnie." "No, No," we said and explained that when you heard the whine you had seven or eight seconds to get into your slit trench before the explosion happened. One of the G.I's looked at us and said that they had taken some casualties as they had never bothered to take cover. I think they did after what we said.

The objective of the 3rd Division was to capture Montisanger, cross the river at Pont de Vaudrey and push through to the main road. The enemy however were using battle-hardened paratroops in good defensive positions to counter this attack. The 9th Infantry Brigade arrived north east of Vire and advanced to connect with the 2nd R.U.R. and the 1st K.O.S.B., with the 2nd Lincolns in reserve – a situation that by now we had come to distrust. Montisanger was cleared by the middle of the afternoon and the battalion advanced to force a bridgehead over the river, the bridge itself having been by now blown up.

The action began at 16.30 hrs, and by 17.15 the two assault companies were successfully across the river, but they had taken casualties in the hard fighting. They advanced further along the heavily-wooded road in failing light. At 23.00 hrs the rest of the battalion was moved across the river, encountering small arms fire and occasional shelling. Around midnight all the companies were over the river in enemy territory. The mortar platoon was in position behind some farm buildings, deploring the loss of our second C.O., Lt Col. Wilson, when we were warned of an impending attack. During the battle we had lost another five men, with thirty-eight wounded.

The next morning Major Colvin returned from Brigade H.Q. with our new C.O., Lt. Col. Firbank of the Somerset Light Infantry and the news that the counter-attack was no longer expected. The advance was to continue. The final aim was still to gain the main road running east from Vire, but the first objective was the railway line. The 2nd Lincolns were given orders to advance, but with no other troops supporting on either flank. D Company which I was with before D-Day was delayed by the enemy holding a sunken road, but A Company advanced steadily and good progress was made.

However, once the whole company had left the cover of the woods for the open cornfields between the wood and the railway, they came under heavy fire from all directions. The enemy were on rising ground beyond the railway, hidden and well equipped with automatic weapons. Advancing any further was impossible without severe casualties and they were finally withdrawn under cover of smoke from the mortar platoon and their own 2 inch mortars.

Meanwhile a platoon from D Company had managed to reach the railway and get one section across, but they immediately came under heavy machine gun and mortar fire from the left flank. Private L. Allison, a platoon runner, was later awarded the Military Medal for extreme courage and devotion to duty by crossing the railway line twice under fire to deliver messages to this isolated section. The company was eventually forced to withdraw, leaving the section which had crossed the railway line to make their way back under cover of darkness, but they were looked for in vain.

When we called the roll, we discovered that we had lost three killed and nineteen wounded, with nine reported missing. One of the fatal casualties was Private. J. Bacon of A Company, who was killed while giving a drink to a wounded comrade. I knew Private Bacon only slightly, but I thought of those words written mostly on the graves of fallen comrades, "Greater love hath no man than this, that he lay down his life for his friends."

We stayed for three more days in the Pont de Vaudrey area, and on 10th August were relieved by the 1st East Yorks and moved east of Vire. Around 18th August we boarded our carriers and moved through Vire to Tinchebray and on to Landisacq, midway between Tinchebray and Flers.

Apart from systematic looting carried out by the retreating army, the village of Landisacq was relatively unscathed. Most of the houses were occupied and other inhabitants returned after we arrived. After several months of witnessing chaos and destruction, this peaceful situation was completely new to us. We settled into the village and were given a friendly welcome. In return we spruced up our appearance and marched through the village in the proper manner as ordered by the officers. What a load of bull! In fact this was the beginning of a month's rest as the battle zone moved further eastwards.

After three days in Landisacq we moved to an area south of Flers, where we stayed until 29th August. There were unfortunately very few billets, so most of the battalion were under canvas. Despite poor weather we remained in good spirits through a programme of training and entertainment, and there was a visit to the theatre in Flers if you were lucky enough to be an officer, to see Flanagan and Allen and the Crazy Gang. We carried out a thorough overhaul of the battalion, checking our kit and motor transport, organised a Battalion Sports Day and attended a concert of music by the band of the Life Guards. We carried out training in river crossing with the intention of putting this into practice when we reached the River Seine. But the Allied advance was so rapid that the Seine was crossed while we were still being trained. However the experience would be put to good use later when we reached the Escaut canal.

On the 29th August the battalion moved a long way east from Flers, across the River Seine to the village of Vatismenil south east of Rouen, where we found ourselves in pleasant countryside with superb weather but still a long way from the front line. On the way we witnessed at first hand the devastating effect of our Allied Air Arm on enemy weapons and transport, the remains of which littered the road for long stretches, especially on the approach to the Seine.

During the stay at Vatismenil the days were long and sunny. We began route marches in columns of three, with the mortar platoon somewhere between C and D Companies. It was during one of these marches that I made a slight mistake. The French countryside that we were passing through contained many orchards full of lovely red apples. Being on the right hand side of the column, which was marching on the right of the road, I was closest to the trees. I remarked to Johnny, our No.1, who was on my left that the apples looked fit to eat and should I grab one or two? Johnny replied that he felt a bit parched what with the dust from the road, so without thinking to check who was behind me, I moved out from the platoon and grabbed two apples. I handed one to Johnny and with great anticipation took a bite out of my apple, thinking of the sweet juices. To my horror it was a bitter taste I was left with. I looked across at Johnny, who with a grin on his face said "cider apples." I threw mine back into the orchard in disgust, when suddenly a voice behind me cried out, "Take that man's name, Sergeant Major." He finally caught up with me, took my name, rank and number and told me I was put on a charge. It appeared that the Adjutant and Sergeant Major had been walking behind us for some time.

The next day I was marched into the company office where sat the Major of S Company and charged with "falling out while on the line of march." I was then asked if I had anything to say. I thought to myself – not a lot and replied "No, sir." "Right, seven days Sergeant Major. March him out." It was called "Jankers." I didn't know why. My punishment was reporting to the guardroom with a "dixie" of tea for the guard who had been on duty all night. I had to fetch the tea from the cookhouse. After seven days of getting up at 6am I returned to normal duties.

Our enjoyable stay at Vatismenil came to an end on 14th September when we set off on the move again. This time we passed the old battlefields of the First World War, crossed over the Somme and through Mons, passing close to the place where my father's youngest brother Oliver was killed all those years ago. [Note : Ray's uncle, Private Oliver James Paine of the 1st/4th Battalion of the King's Shropshire Light Infantry was killed in the Third Battle of the Aisne in World War 1 on Friday 31 May 1918, aged 29. He has no known grave but his name is recorded on the British Memorial at Soissons, north east France.] We stopped for the night near Soignies and after having a brew-up and some food we bedded down for the night in some farm buildings. Two of us made a hole in the haystack pushing our way in and fell fast asleep.

In the morning we washed and had breakfast when the shout came, "Start up!" We quickly threw things into the carrier and the crew got into their seats. Soon we were moving on past the British Lion mounting guard over the field of Waterloo, through Louvain, and north across the Albert Canal to an area south of St. Hubert, Lille. From here we could hear the sounds of battle once more. The battalion's first task was to carry out an assault crossing of a water obstacle – the Escaut Canal, which here ran east to west. The bridge over the canal had been blown up by the enemy and the 3rd Division was called into action to force a crossing of the canal so that the Engineers could bridge it, for the 11th Armoured Division to then advance into Holland.

The battalion arrived south of the canal on the afternoon of 16th September, with the 2nd Lincolns settling into a wooded area on the right of the main road. The assault was originally planned for the night of 19th/20th September, but it was brought forward to midnight on the 18th. The 2nd R.U.R. were to cross to the left of the demolished bridge with the 2nd Lincolns on the right. Following the successful crossing, the 1st K.O.S.B. would then pass through, establish the bridgehead and advance towards the village of Achel.

The canal itself was particularly difficult to cross under fire. On either side were steep banks rising to ten feet above the surrounding countryside and over the banks there was a six foot drop down a concrete wall to water level. Just before midnight the artillery began firing at the opposite bank, to be met by enemy mortar fire. At midnight the boats were lowered and despite further heavy fire from small arms and a 20mm gun firing directly along the canal the two companies successfully reached the other side by 00.15 hours.

The enemy retreated after setting fire to a house on the opposite bank, illuminating the whole area now swarming with boats and men. All of the rifle companies were across the canal by 02.15 hours, D Company and forward Battalion HQ were established in the village of Broek and by dawn the class 12 bridge had been completed by the Engineers.

On the following day the 1st K.O.S.B. were advancing slowly along the main road towards Achel against relatively light enemy resistance. However, A Company were facing much more serious resistance from a determined force of officer cadets and it was not until late afternoon that the Germans finally retreated.

It was in this area that, while our mortars were firing on a target a mile away, our section launched a round which went wrong. As we watched the flight of the mortar from out of the barrel, we saw its tail fin fall off. Without the tail the bomb turns over and over in the air, coming down well short of the target. We watched in horror as it landed among some soldiers in front of us and we feared the worst. One of our sergeants went over to find out and came back with the good news that the soldiers had heard the funny noise the bomb was making on the way down and dived for cover. Luckily they all dived different ways which helped and because of the sandy nature of the ground, the bomb went deep before it exploded. Only one man was injured when a lump of hot shrapnel landed on his backside as he dived for cover – a very lucky man.

The battalion advanced on 20th September to reach a monastery east of Achel, where the monks eventually revealed that the building had been used as a German HQ. Casualties suffered during the Escaut Canal operation were three officers killed and fifty-nine other ranks wounded.

Chapter Five
Battle of Venraij

On 21st September the battalion moved east of Achel to a small town called Hamont, and on 26th September we moved on again and crossed the border to relieve the 3rd Monmouths in the Dutch town of Deurne. Large numbers of airborne troops had been dropped at Arnhem and Nijmegen and the supply lines needed protection.

We were moving up to Veghel when the Germans cut the main supply line twice and we had to fight to re-open it. The traffic was not able to resume movement until the following day. I remember being cut off and short of food, when somewhere nearby they found a warehouse with German rations inside. The provisions were handed out to the column of vehicles, and the army lived off German frankfurters (a small smoked sausage). I seem to remember them as very spicy. Ugh!

In Deurne we tested the German line of defences along the canal and then, after four days, we moved to the area between Bakel and Milheeze. Finally we moved nearer to the River Maas, some being stationed in the village of Oeffelt and the remainder in the area of Haps. Here we stayed until 11th October with no major incident occurring. The mortar platoon was stationed in a farm building and we made ourselves quite at home. When we tried to dig our mortar pits in the field, we got no further than six inches before they filled up with water! The only place we could find to stand the mortars in was a six foot concrete ring in the farmyard.

With the loss of the bridge at Arnhem operations shifted towards Aachen, already occupied by the American 3rd Army, and Venlo, gateway to the Ruhr. The British 3rd Division moved south to take part in this operation with the plan of clearing the east bank of the River Maas southwards to Venraij.

Following a delay caused by bad weather the battalion left Haps on 11th October and moved to an area east of St. Anthonis. The 8th British Infantry Brigade were already attacking the village of Overloon and we could hear the thunder of artillery as we moved nearer. Before nightfall Overloon had been captured and forward positions had been established.

On Friday 13th October the brigade advanced with the 2nd R.U.R. and the 1st K.O.S.B. leading, and the 2nd Lincolns in the rear. We took up a position to the north of Overloon and awaited the order to advance. South of Overloon was a wooded area and beyond that were open fields and the small village of Venraij. The battle plan was to clear the woods of the enemy, advance across the open countryside and capture Venraij. However, the area was heavily mined and the open fields were under observation by the enemy from the church tower in Venraij. The significance of the date was not lost on us and the battalion was destined to suffer heavy casualties in the ensuing battle.

The task of the 2nd R.U.R. was to clear the eastern half of the wood, with the 1st K.O.S.B. clearing the western side. The 2nd Lincolns would then pass through, cross the open ground and a water-filled ditch and clear the second wood. Little was known about the ditch so a patrol set out at 04.00 to carry out a reconnoitre. However this was unsuccessful and B Company under Major A.J. Smith set off at dawn without any information on how serious an obstacle it was.

But the small arms fire from the wood was deceptive and when the company was out in the open and approaching the ditch they were suddenly faced with heavy artillery fire from the enemy. So many casualties were taken that any further advance was impossible. Major Smith ordered the mortar platoon to put down smoke and withdrew his men. Following such a disastrous start, plans were then devised to carry out a full scale battalion attack with tanks protecting the right flank. The attack would commence at 15.30 hours.

The mortar platoon at this time was moving to get into position along a track leading into a wood when the leading carrier was suddenly lifted on its side by a terrific explosion. The second carrier stopped and the men went forward to help the wounded. The third carrier, containing Johnny Goodson, myself and two others were told to stop where we were as there were mines everywhere. Our driver was ordered to back out, keeping in the tracks we had made on advancing. Just to the left we came across a jeep which had been blown over on its side and both occupants killed. In our lead carrier, two men were wounded and one man died half an hour later in the First Aid Post. With all this happening and knowing that the first attack had been forced to withdraw, there was an uneasy and apprehensive feeling amongst us on this overcast and dull day. This uneasy feeling was to prove only too well justified.

At 15.30 hours our barrage came down and the advance began. As expected, we were faced with heavy artillery fire, but this time there was no retreating. Despite many casualties the companies advanced in a determined fashion to capture the wood. Any Germans remaining in the wood threw down their weapons and ran.

We cleared our section of the wood and dug in, remaining there for two days, during which time we experienced only occasional shelling. More of a problem were the Schu-mines which caused many casualties. On 16th October the 1st Suffolks passed through to take part in the attack on Venraij and we moved back to the area that we had come from.

After the battle the C.O. Lt-Col C.L.Fairbanks was awarded the DSO for his part in the operation, for personal bravery and devotion to duty in the front line. The D.C.M. was awarded to my old C.S.M. W. Shaw of D Company, who I knew from my days with them when training in Scotland.

It was while in this area around Overloon in a lull in the fighting that the mortar platoon was ordered to help the Pioneers fill in a river with rubble to enable vehicles to cross. In Overloon there were plenty of buildings in ruins, so with shovels and a three ton truck we were told to report to the school and proceeded to load the lorry with bricks from the rubble of the school ruins, which were then transported during darkness and with the minimum of noise to the river. We were told that the enemy were somewhere over the river, so whilst some stood guard the rest of us started unloading. The noise we made was awful and the exertion made us sweat. We were sure that the enemy would open fire and kill us all! The lorry was unloaded in very quick time and we all piled on and drove back to the school where we thought we had finished for the night. However we were told to start loading up again! Nothing happened that night – secretly I think they told us that the enemy were close by to make us hurry up – but we were glad to get back to our own area in the morning. It seemed that we got on so well with the Pioneers and we were doing little at the time that they requested our services again.

About two weeks later the Pioneers had orders to lay mines between two woods in front of the duty companies, who were dug in, to stop any threat of tanks or vehicles breaking through. We met the same men we had helped before and loaded the mines, which were in heavy steel boxes, into the back of the three-ton truck. Then off we went on a cold, moonlit night along a track for about half a mile and then drove very slowly to keep the noise down to a point behind the wood. The sergeant in charge told us that we were about half a mile from the enemy position, and to remember not to drop the handles of the mine's cases as there would be a loud bang. We were very careful I can tell you!

We then had to carry one box of mines between two men and up the side of the wood and stack them ready to be laid. We also moved some further away from the trees. The sergeant thanked us and told us that we had completed our task. We thankfully left them to it. Mines which explode and leave a large hole were certainly not our "cup of tea." The moon at this time had vanished behind clouds and as we had left the Pioneers well behind us we couldn't very well ask them for directions. We began to feel lost and very uneasy. One of us said we should go this way, whilst another came up with a completely different direction. All the woods and trees seemed the same, with no landmarks to guide us. One of the platoon said that he felt sure this was the way, so we all followed him, hoping that he had a better sense of direction than the rest of us, when the moon suddenly re-appeared from behind a bank of cloud. I stood there looking for the Plough and the Pole Star in the night sky, as then I knew where north was. We knew we needed to go west, but we had actually been travelling east! There was still some uncertainty and hesitation, but when I said that I was going this way and if anyone wished to go the other they would finish up in a prisoner of war camp, everyone fell in behind and after fifteen minutes we found the road and made our way back thankfully to our area near Overloon.

Chapter Six
Leave In Brussels and England

Following its withdrawal from the battle between Overloon and Venraij on 16th October, the battalion would now spend over four months before seriously encountering the enemy again. This time was spent in the wooded country west of the river Maas, around Venraij and in occupying different sectors of the Maas.

It was whilst in this area that the battalion had the honour to be chosen as the "typical fighting County Regiment" to take part in a broadcast service for Armistice Day. The service took place at Oploo, between Overloon and St. Anthonis on Sunday November 5th and was broadcast from a recording the following Saturday. Our padre, Captain (Rev) D. Wynne Jones read the prayers, the lesson was read by the C.O. Lt. Col. Firbank D.S.O. and the address was given by Rev. J.W.J. Steele, the Hampshire cricketer.

On 20th November the battalion moved from the rest area at St Anthonis to Veulen, a small village south west of Venraij, where we relieved the 3rd Monmouths of the 11th Armoured Division. The enemy held most of the surrounding woods but when we advanced to attack three days later we found that they had withdrawn on the previous day. We discovered later that the enemy had left a minimum force in place in the north in order to concentrate their forces on the Ardennes offensive.

During our time in the Venraij area the platoon were dug in near a comfortable farmhouse. One day my mate Charlie Smith and I were in the farmhouse having eaten, writing letters. Charlie left the room after finishing his letter and returned some minutes later and calmly put down on the table in front of me a little square wooden box. "Joe (this was my nickname in the army), look what I've found," he said. I took another look and jumped up in horror as I realised it was a German Schu-mine, which had been responsible for many Allied casualties. Our mine detectors failed to pick them up as they were made of wood and dovetailed so there was no metal to register. Outside the farmhouse down a slope to the riverbank where Charlie had walked, the Germans had buried them just under the sandy soil. During the night it had rained heavily and this had washed the soil off the top of the lids. Charlie had been a very lucky chap! We had been issued with what we called prodders, which were sticks about four feet long. The idea was that you should lie on your stomach and prod the ground at arm's length in front of you. Thank goodness we were spared from doing that as the sergeant formed a line of us to pick the mines up, being very careful not to close the lids. I forget how many we picked up along the riverbank, but I was glad it had rained the previous night as any one of us could have walked into them otherwise.

At about this time short periods of leave in Brussels had been arranged. My turn came up for forty-eight hours leave a week before Christmas and I travelled in with a lad called Freddy. On arriving in Brussels, we found that all the hotels were full, but we could take advantage of a scheme whereby civilians would give us bed and breakfast and arrange for lunch in a restaurant. We were taken to the nominated street and given the house number and I walked up the steps of a four-storey house. Freddy was housed in a similar place next door. I rang the bell, wondering who I was about to meet. The door was opened by a young lady, who kindly invited me to step inside. She said she was Miss Morritt's maid and asked me to follow her upstairs to meet the lady herself. At the top of the stairs was a very large landing and a large door, leading into a massive room with a very high ceiling. The sides of the room were taken up with bookcases all filled from floor to ceiling. In the corner near the window there was a large bed, with a table next to it, and in a wheelchair next to the bed sat a lady, who welcomed me to Brussels in English (which took me aback) and said that she hoped I would enjoy my stay. Asking me to take a seat nearby she enquired where I had come from and where I lived in England. The maid arrived with tea and cakes. We continued our conversation. She originally came from Barnard Castle just over the Yorkshire border and had moved to France just before the 2nd World War. When the Germans overran France she became very frightened but was determined not to leave her home, which overlooked a river. She knew that when the Germans arrived the British Army would defend it to the last minute and the house would probably be destroyed. A British officer contacted her and tried to persuade her to move to a safer place, but she was adamant, and with true British grit (and stubbornness) insisted that she remain, even if it was the death of her. At this point in the conversation she suddenly apologised and said that she was keeping me from my comrade next door. I was about to advise her to the contrary when the maid knocked and entered the room to say there was a soldier at the door and was I ready to go out? Before I left I was shown my room and bathroom and advised that I would be woken at 08.00 for breakfast. I thanked the lady for our talk which I had thoroughly enjoyed, and she invited me to have some more conversation before I left.

Freddy and I went out to find the restaurant where we had tickets for lunch the next day. It was quite a distance away, so after a few beers we decided to take the tram back, which would drop us at the end of the road near to our billets. The tram car was nearly full of passengers, but when they saw that we were soldiers they made room for us. They anxiously enquired if we thought that the Germans would re-invade Brussels. The war situation at this time was very tense with the Germans breaking the American lines, so to reassure them we said that Monty wouldn't let them down – and hoped we were right! Just as we said this the sirens started in the distance and overhead the noise of a doodle bug, or flying bomb, came chugging over. Suddenly it cut out and everything went deathly quiet, both in the sky and in the tram car. The people of Brussels had endured these bombs for quite a while and reacted by throwing themselves on the floor around our feet, with Freddy and me still standing. By the time Freddy and I decided we should join them, the bomb went off two or three streets away with a deafening roar. After that, everyone on the floor started to rise and brush the dust off their clothes and regain their composure. We asked someone where to get off, as it was a blackout and found our way back. Our first night in the Belgian capital – and we hoped no more flying bombs.

In the morning someone tapped on my door and said that breakfast would be ready in half an hour. After breakfast I called round for Freddy and we visited the sights of Brussels and had a lovely lunch at the restaurant. We visited one of the Army and Navy clubs and generally had a nice restful day. The time seemed to pass very quickly and on my last day with the great old lady, she invited me into her room for one last chat. I commented on all the books in her library, a lot of which were written by Sir Walter Scott and I seem to recall that she told me that she was a distant relative. She also told me that she was the founder of the British Empire Shakespeare Society in 1901 and its first Honorary Secretary. She let me look at the original pamphlet, which showed the president to be Sir Henry Irving and the address of Miss Greta Morritt as 17, Southwell Gardens, S.W. London. Before we said our goodbyes she gave me a small book of the play "As You Like It." At the front of the book on the fly-leaf she had written "To Raymond Paine Brussels 1944 from Greta Morritt, founder of B.E.S.S.

1901." I was very proud to meet such a great lady. I wrote to her after the war when I arrived back from Palestine, but my letter was returned address not known, so I assumed she must have died.

We left Brussels and arrived back in Horst just two days before Christmas. At the beginning of December we had received news that home leave was to commence from 1st January. Some people would rather have got everything over with first but most welcomed the prospect of a week of glorious bliss. The battalion was divided into groups based on the embarkation dates from England and a series of ballots was held.

During the Christmas period we were billeted with a family in Horst, which was a peaceful enough area. The family consisted of the two parents, two sons who had been hidden under the floorboards when the Germans came looking for slave labour, and a young girl called Nellie. We all slept in one room and the family slept in the other. Food was scarce at the time, so we gave them some tins of corned beef, baked beans and soup. One of the corporals provided some whisky and rum and all of us had a lovely Christmas. Before we left Horst ready to move into Germany, Nellie gave me a photograph of herself as we said goodbye – I wonder if she survived the war?

At the beginning of January I was told to pack my kit and was given my leave pass at company office. Along with twenty or so other men I piled into a lorry which took us to the nearest railway station, from where we took the train to Calais. We had a very rough crossing and were relieved to get off at Folkestone.

We were warned by tannoy on the boat that if we were found to be carrying unauthorised weapons, such as German Luger pistols, when going through Customs, we would be sent straight back to the front. Many littered Folkestone harbour with their treasures of war. The train was already standing in Folkestone harbour when we disembarked and was soon filled with troops eager to get home. The whistle was blown and we moved slowly out of the station up the very steep incline, the engine initially being helped by a tank engine at the back. Breasting the rise and looking back down on the white cliffs made me think how lucky we were to see our "green and pleasant land" again.

I enjoyed every minute of the train journey, and especially relished the baked beans on toast and mug of tea from the Y.M.C.A. near St. Pancras station. A feast indeed! The train journey to Kettering took over two hours and when I arrived there was no connection to Desborough. I therefore collected up my gas mask, backpack and rifle and walked up to the bus depot at the top of Northampton Road. I stood around for quite a while until an old lady came past and remarked, "They stop running at 9 o'clock, me duck!" So I made up my mind to walk, thinking that it wasn't far and anyway I could always thumb it. I reached a point about a mile from Rothwell, not having seen a single car, when in the distance I heard the sound of a motorbike about on its last legs. I didn't thumb it, as it struggled to pass me, but the rider on the bike and sidecar yelled, "Do you want a lift?" I replied, "No thanks" and he disappeared out of sight. Rounding the next bend into Rothwell, just by the junction with the road to Loddington, this fellow was on his knees tinkering with the engine and not seeming to get much response!

I arrived in Desborough at about midnight and took the short cut through the "Dams" by the church. That hill nearly finished me off and I was ready for a good night's sleep when I arrived back at 58 Queen Street. Mother greeted me and was worried that I was so late. I told the tale over a refreshing cup of tea. Sleeping in my own bed that night was just great, thinking as I closed my eyes that there would be no stand-to on guard tomorrow!

Whilst on leave I visited Vi Stephenson and her mother who lived in East Ham, where I stopped for the night. During the day I went up to the West End and had a meal at the Lyons Corner House. After that I went over to King's Cross and decided to watch a film in the cinema opposite the station. The film showing was called "Thirty Seconds over Tokyo" and was about the first raid by carrier-borne aircraft on the Japanese capital. The planes were approaching the city about to drop their load when the cinema was shook by a large explosion, frightening everyone inside including me. I wondered at that time if I wouldn't be safer back in the front line! The dust fell on us from out of the roof, but otherwise we were all OK. The management of the cinema put a notice up on the screen to say that people were at liberty to leave, but the film would continue. I don't remember anyone leaving and most saw the end of the film. The movietone news clip which followed the film was called "London can take it" and was about the V2 rockets raining down on our capital city. Leaving the cinema, I turned left into Euston Road and left again into Argyll Street to find the area a hundred yards ahead cordoned off, with the Fire Service and First Aid in attendance. A V2 rocket had ripped right through a six or seven storey block of flats. I can safely say that I wouldn't have liked to have been any nearer.

At the beginning of January there were very strong gales in the Channel and my leave was extended by seventy-two hours as a consequence. We were told to listen to the news on the radio if this happened and the ferries were stopped. We were all given a leave number and if you heard your number you had another twenty-four hours' leave. I was very lucky and had two cancelled. The journey back down to the coast through London on a dull, wet and windy day was helped by the company of two other Army men returning. We had all hoped that during our time on leave the Germans would somehow give way and surrender. But it was not to be. Indeed the Germans were fighting harder as they were pushed back onto their home soil.

Charlie Smith, Ray's best friend

Ray in mortar pit with 3" mortar, Barnstorf 11 April 1945.

Mortar platoon, Barnstoft April 1945

Ray in wagon, Barnstorf 9 April 1945

Ray in Belgium October 1945

Ray in Lengerich, 9 May 1945

Ray, top left, in Hadera, Palestine, late 1945

Charlie and Mac on train

Bremen Airfield where the last mortar bombs were fired

Ray, top left, bricklaying

Ray and Audrey's wedding, 26 June 1948

Left to Right: Joan Crick, Charlie Smith, Mabel Paine, Ray, Rosemary Tailby, Audrey, Colin Crick, Florrie Crick, Joyce Crick

Chapter Seven
Entering Germany

When I arrived back we were stationed in the area of Smakt and Lottum, tiny Dutch villages on or near the banks of the river, pleasant and prosperous no doubt in days of peace, but in war broken and forlorn, with every church or tall building in utter ruin and every day a target for the enemy defences on the Siegfried Line. At Smakt we used the same houses as the Germans had used for observation posts and looked down on our previous positions in the woods. How close they were, and how evident every unguarded movement must have been. We realised how grateful we were for the comparative deficiency of the German artillery, and our policy of hitting back strongly every time he dared shoot at us.

Whilst we were in this area it was really cold, and the ground was mostly covered in snow and ice. I had done something wrong again (I can't remember what!) and had been allocated seven days' "Jankers." One of my allotted duties was to run messages to any one of the duty companies who were stationed on the banks of the river Maas. We slept in farm buildings, but it was so cold that we slept fully clothed. One day I was woken at about 04.00 and given a message to take to the company on the river line. I put on my jerkin and balaclava and set off into the pitch black, with the sergeant's last words ringing in my ear, "There have been German patrols in the area, so watch your step." There was a small track that I tried to follow with a small river on my left which would lead me to the company. I have never felt so cold and lonely in my life. I remembered to put a "round up the spout" and left my safety catch off. How long the journey took I could not say, but I was glad to hear someone call to me to halt from the corner of a farm building. He was as cold as I was.

One of the men took me to a room in the farm, where an officer sat at a table drinking tea. Saluting, I gave him the message. After a moment he looked at me, asked me to sit down and offered me a cup of tea. He asked if I would like to read the message I had just delivered. Thinking that it probably warned of an impending enemy attack, I picked it up and read as follows; "Owing to a lot of enemy activity from over the river, in future men will move around in pairs. Anybody disobeying this will be severely punished." I looked across to the lieutenant, who was laughing quietly at the look of horror on my face. Having finished my tea the officer told me to hurry back as it would be light in thirty minutes and the track I took was shelled most mornings at first light. Thanking him I started back out full of trepidation, and the lighter it got the quicker I tried to go. After I passed the stretch that had been shelled before I felt much better, but before I arrived back at our billet I heard a few bangs in that area. Arriving back I was relieved to get inside the farm buildings because I was so cold, and soon got my head down.

A short time after I finished my "sentence" I went back to normal soldiering. It was still intensely cold, as only Holland can be. Charlie Smith and I were on guard duty outside the farmhouse, where we had built a shelter out of ammunition boxes, hoping to keep out the keen wind. We were keeping watch on the track leading away from us. Now and again we would patrol, if only to keep our feet warm! Suddenly we heard a noise in the distance like a low flying plane coming straight towards us. Charlie dived into a small ditch and I followed him (luckily the ditch was frozen solid) and the thing went over us with fire belching out the back of it. Back on our feet, we realised that what we had seen was a doodlebug fired from enemy lines on its way to Antwerp or some similar target. Guard duties at this time were only of half an hour duration due to the intense cold. Before we started our duty the sergeant always put a generous dash of rum in our mugs of tea, which gave you a warm glow inside. However by the time you had been outside for ten minutes, the feeling had gone and you were always glad to be relieved.

On 7th February the battalion left the west bank of the Maas and moved to Wilsele, a small village about three miles north of Leuven, where the villagers showed us a lot of hospitality which will never be forgotten. We stayed for just over two weeks and couldn't have been happier. Two sections of the mortar platoon were billeted with a family consisting of a husband, wife and teenage son, with whom we used to play cards. In the kitchen at the back of the house was an enormous stove that the wife used to cook on, coming out nearly into the centre of the room. On top of this she had an enamel bath tin, about two feet across, and in this she used to cook the most delicious soup, full of vegetables from the garden. We all had second helpings and then slept comfortably in their lounge.

On the second evening we returned to the house and she had made another bath tin full again. Retiring to our sleeping place we all wondered how she was managing to make so much. At the time of the German occupation the Belgian people were very short of food and we soon realised that at the rate we were eating, these people would have little left when we departed. We had a cookhouse in the same street, so after breakfast I went and asked if they had a spare tin of "bully." Someone handed me a couple of tins. Evening came round and I went to the good lady and gave her my tins. I think she was quite overwhelmed as four or five of my comrades had also arrived with cans of soup, beef stew and yet more bully! We all had plenty of cans of food on the carrier which we left with her when we departed.

On 24th February we moved east and crossed the River Maas at Gennep, to play our part in "Operation Veritable." The objective was to clear the enemy from the country between the Maas and the Rhine. The operation had begun on 8th February and good progress had been made despite difficult terrain in the Reichswald Forest and large flooded areas.

We received orders to relieve the 7th Argyll and Sutherland Highlanders south east of Goch and in the evening the battalion finally entered Germany itself. The immediate objective was to clear the enemy from a wooded area and then capture the villages of Kervenheim and Winnekendonk, ready for an armoured advance. The 2nd Lincolns were called into action at 04.00 on the morning of 27th February. We moved forward to a sunken track screened by bushes and advanced at 07.30 towards a wooded area near a small village.

We were surprised at the light resistance and achieved our objective with some ease. For the first time we came across large numbers of German officers and men who immediately gave themselves up as we arrived. This was unexpected but became increasingly common as we advanced, marking the beginning of the defeat of Germany.

The 28th February was spent resting and in the evening we came under the command of 185 Brigade to assist in the capture of Kervenheim. At 06.00 hours on 1st March we set off and by 07.30 we were in position for the attack. This went well initially and by mid-morning we had reached the village where the fighting increased in intensity and weather conditions deteriorated rapidly with rain falling on already saturated ground. This made any further advance very difficult. A determined push against stubborn resistance finally cleared the factory area at the north of the village and we gained a foothold on the main road from Uedem. No further progress was made after dark but enemy resistance was broken and the village was successfully captured in the morning, with the whole battalion concentrated in the southern outskirts by 14.00.

The final objective was still the capture of Winnekendonk, and this was to be completed as soon as possible after 17.00. Information gathered from prisoners of war suggested that Winnekendonk and the woods behind the village were held by a weak battalion. We had advanced to the position at which we were ready to attack at the appointed time but still no artillery or tank support had materialised. We waited and then at last the barrage began. The order to attack was given and as we moved forward the Churchill tanks arrived in the nick of time. We now emerged from the wood onto open ground where we were met with heavy machine gun fire and anti-tank guns. Two tanks were hit and many men fell as the battalion surged forward under relentless fire. By 18.20 we had reached the road junction near the village, but were still under fire from snipers and machine guns. As we entered the village the savage fighting continued until the Germans were finally killed, wounded or surrendered.

We remained in Winnekendonk for ten days, stationed in an area on the outskirts of the village. A number of houses were showing the white flag and, amongst the strewn contents, we saw hundreds of photographs of Nazi propaganda. Our total casualties in the operation were two officers and fifteen other ranks killed, four officers and eighty-two other ranks wounded, and six other ranks missing. An old friend of mine deployed in D Company, Corporal Spye, won the Military Medal.

On 13ᵗʰ March we moved to take over a sector of the River Rhine, first at Hochend and then to an area around Obermürmter. Here there was a pall of thick smoke on the west bank designed to obscure the enemy's view of our preparations for the river crossing. The mortar platoon in this period was stationed in an area around a vicarage. We were all able to sleep in the vicarage cellar, which was warm and dry. Charlie Smith and I always paired up for guard duties. For three nights we had the 10pm to midnight shift, and the arched gateway to the vicarage garden provided a welcome refuge if it happened to be wet. On the fourth night our shift was changed to the 8pm to 10pm shift. After completing it we returned to the cellar, which served as a guardroom, and had fallen asleep when we were woken by a large explosion. As all went quiet we fell asleep again. Just before 2am we were told that it was time for our next shift. We accordingly relieved our two comrades and started our guard duties. As we walked down the lane and came to our gateway all we could see was a load of rubble. I looked at Charlie and said that if we had been on our usual shift we would have been flattened! And so it turned out for we later found out that the explosion occurred at around 11.30pm. We both felt very lucky again.

Chapter Eight
The Battle of Bremen

The 3rd Division took no direct part in the crossing of the Rhine but we certainly heard a huge amount of artillery fire during the operation. The troops began to cross in Buffaloes at 21.00 hours under the light of the moon and found the enemy positions on the far bank exactly as had been expected from observations and interrogation of prisoners of war. The following morning saw the arrival of a massive Airborne Force heading for the rear of the German defences.

On the afternoon of 28th March the battalion crossed the River Rhine at Rees and settled in an area south of the town, where our objective was to capture the town of Haldern and the high ground to the north. Early on 29th March the K.O.S.B. advanced as far as Werth where they found that the bridge over the Oude Issel had been destroyed. B Company then pushed forward to find out whether the bridges at Lensing and Doing had been blown, and the remainder of the battalion moved forward to Monkerai.

Finding that the bridge at Lensing was blown, it was decided that a full-scale Brigade attack should be launched against the German positions, with the first assault at 01.00 and the second at 05.00. The attack went very well and all objectives were captured by 04.00.

A few days of rest followed until April 2nd which saw us on the move again. The night was spent in Groenlo, and it was a pleasant change to be back in the country where flags of liberation were flying and the people glad to see us. The following day took us to Enschede, where we only stopped for a short while but were soon encircled by the Dutch people who had come out of their homes to greet us. Thankfully they almost all spoke English! Some of them invited us into their kitchens to share a celebration drink. I was invited in by a grey-haired old lady, who was in tears with emotion. I took a tin of stew out of the pack on the carriers and gave it to her, which brought more tears. We toasted Holland and then the Army, before the call came to start up and move off. As I said goodbye to her she pressed a small Dutch coin, very bright, into my hand and said, "You keep that and when you look at it think of me and Holland." I ran out of the house and climbed on the carrier which was ready to move off. As a bricklayer I admired the neat brickwork of their lovely houses which had dormer windows in every roof. However, there was more serious business ahead as we advanced to Oldenzaal on April 4th and across the German border to a concentration area near the small village of Südlohne.

The enemy were holding out in the small town of Lingen on the far bank of the Dortmund-Ems canal and the battalion was moved to the centre of Lingen in an area already captured and held by the 1st Royal Norfolk. Here we were faced with street fighting in the dark without the benefit of reconnaissance or prior knowledge of enemy positions. Progress was slow and the enemy had no intention of withdrawing.

The following morning however was more successful. Supported now by tanks and crocodiles (flame-throwers) we attacked with such vigour that within a very short time the enemy were either captured or had retreated.

The mortar platoon was moved into an area in the town near a school, setting up the mortars on a lawn nearby. Whilst waiting for orders we had a look in the cellars of the school building and found that the Germans had been using it as an H.Q. Having left in a hurry, there was quite a bit of equipment left behind, and by the time we moved forward most of the carriers had a typewriter on board! Lingen cost the battalion four other ranks and one officer killed, with seventeen other ranks wounded.

The 2nd Lincolns were now called upon for the first phase of opening up the Lingen-Plantlünne axis, but this passed off without incident, the enemy having no heart to defend the country to the south following the rout in Lingen. The following evening we moved into the village of Polle Estringen Rottum after the 2nd R.U.R and 1st K.O.S.B had cleared it. During the night some young boys of the Hitler Youth Movement planted a mine under one of the carriers. When the carrier moved off, its track exploded the mine, throwing the vehicle on its side. The officer in charge immediately threw a cordon round the houses, which were all searched for arms. Some guns were taken away with a stern warning to the people concerned that this would not be tolerated.

The battalion was suddenly switched at a moment's notice from one Corps to another. We were told the following day that we should move to an area in the neighbourhood of Ostercappeln, some seven or eight miles north-east of Osnabrück. In fact, once we were on the move we did not stop until we had passed some fifty miles beyond that point. We finally settled down in the small township of Barnstorf on the Osnabrück-Bremen road, about twenty miles south west of Bremen. At Barnstorf, and later at Reckum and Kleineköhren, we were allocated a defensive role on the left flank of the 7th Armoured Division, and then on 17th April we moved to an area south of Brinkum ready for a Brigade attack on the outer defences of Bremen itself.

These defences were positioned in a series of small villages around Bremen, separated from the city itself by low-lying flooded ground where there was little cover from automatic weapons. Furthermore this area was visible from many tall buildings in Bremen. During the operation it reminded many of us of the time in Normandy and the Colombelles chimneys. It was at this point that we began to realise that the end of the war was not far away and we became more on edge, always looking for the nearest slit-trench to jump into when we moved about in case danger threatened. The possibility that we had survived this far only to get killed in the last days of the war truly did not bear thinking about!

Brinkum and Kirchweyne, due south of Bremen, had already been captured and our own Brigade were called into action at 06.00 to take Stuhr, Moordeich, Mittelshuchting and Kirchhuchting. It was a long and difficult day, but the enemy had insufficient artillery support and retreated in the face of the onslaught. More ground was captured on the morning of the following day. On 20th April the battalion attacked Kirchhuchting and before nightfall we had succeeded in capturing it, and had crossed the railway line running due east from Delmenhorst to Bremen.

The final objective was the capture of Bremen south and east of the river Weser and on 21st April the 9th Brigade was moved away from the battle to prepare. The battalion spent four days in the unspoilt village of Ristedt, eight or nine miles further south. While we were there the British press began to publish photographs and details of the horrific conditions in the concentration camps at Belsen and Buchenwald. The Commanding Officer decided that this should be brought to the attention of the local inhabitants, who were then shown the pictures with a written explanatory note.

At midnight on the 24th/25th April, the 2nd R.U.R. started the attack to capture Bremen. Using Buffaloes to cross the flooded area between Brinkum and the Ochtum canal, they captured the bridge at Kattenturm by 05.00. Then the 1st K.O.S.B. followed through and reached an important road junction two thousand yards beyond the bridge. We were still under fire from the airfield and the Focke-Wulf works over to the left, and the Lincolns were called into action to attack these areas. The attack began at

14.00 hours and despite some heavy fighting all objectives had been achieved by 17.30.

The mortar platoon itself had moved into the area of the Focke-Wulf works. This turned out to be where we fired the last mortar bombs of the war in Europe. Nearby were German planes which had been bombed in the last weeks of the war and also very large bomb shelters about sixty feet high and shaped like a huge bomb on end.

The casualties in the battle for Bremen had been comparatively light, but included Lt. W.C. Piper, a platoon commander in C Company who was killed by a sniper - almost the very last shot fired against us. On 27th April we moved to Delmenhorst, a small town five miles west of Bremen.

Chapter Nine
War Officially Over

During the next few days we were moving in convoy. It was a lovely sunny day around midday with the sun high in the sky, when we noticed that part of it was getting darker and we realised that we were seeing an eclipse of the sun. The convoy came to an abrupt halt and we dismounted and stood around, taking turns with someone's dark glasses to observe this phenomenon. It turned out to be a total eclipse, where so much sunlight is shut out that darkness falls just as if the sun had set. At that moment all the birds stopped singing and we stopped talking, and it seemed that the world had stopped for that moment in time. It held us all spellbound. I shall never forget that feeling. Nor will I forget the sun becoming brighter again and the birds recommencing their song.

On 7th May the battalion left Delmenhorst for Lengerich, a pretty little village ten miles south-west of Osnabrück. When we left Delmenhorst we knew that the end of the war was near and we were in a relaxed and happy mood. On the journey we were suddenly brought to a halt by a soldier running out into the middle of the road, waving a bottle about and shouting, "It's all over!" More men came out of a building and we celebrated with them. I walked down to meet Charlie Smith, who had just got down from his carrier. We shook hands, our eyes full of tears of emotion, celebrating that we had made it - then, almost instantaneously, feeling guilty about those who had not survived. Someone thrust a bottle of beer into our hands and we drank to our fallen comrades. Suddenly the cry went up, "Mount carriers" and we had to continue our journey to Lengerich. We said goodbye to our hosts and thanked them for the liquid refreshments! Truly a day to remember forever.

At Lengerich the mortar platoon was billeted in a large house overlooked by high ground at the rear. We all settled in well and apart from guard duties relaxed in the knowledge that we could have a good night's sleep. Whilst we were there the 2nd Army held a Thanksgiving Service on the conclusion of the campaign in North-West Europe and to remember those who had given their lives.

After a few weeks we were moved to the Ruhr, which had been extensively bombed by the R.A.F. and the U.S.A.F. to the point of devastation. We were billeted in a building formerly used by S.S. troops in the town of Recklinghausen. From here we undertook guard duties in a camp housing Italian prisoners of war. After the war had finished they had roamed the countryside killing the German farmers' cows for food and generally making nuisances of themselves. We got on very well with them generally and tried to keep a bit of order. They had their own band and later we discovered that they had girlfriends in the barracks with them. Truly all home comforts! After a while they started getting a bit naughty again and we decided that we would make them parade and take a count of heads. We finally managed to get them all on the parade ground, but failed to get them to line up for the count as they were all chatting and acting as if they couldn't be bothered. Five of us had rifles and one had a Sten gun with a full magazine. He emptied the magazine into the air above the head of the Italians. I have never seen so many men move so quickly and in panic to form three lines so that we could count them!

After about three or four weeks the time came to move again – this time nearer to Brussels. We were given a grim reminder that the Japanese were still fighting and had to be beaten before the war could be said to be over. The rumour going around was that the 3rd Division was to be an assault Division and would be given the same job they had performed on D-Day, but this time on the Japanese mainland. We were in a very sombre mood, as we knew that each Japanese soldier would fight to the death. We were eventually told that we would be flying to Oxford and would have four weeks' leave before joining up with the 1st Guards Brigade and the U.S. Army in Kentucky, ready to undertake the assault on Japan. We were in rather a large billet on 13th August when the sergeant came in and told us to get our heads down, as reveille would be at 04:00. This would enable us to have breakfast, get our kit packed and be transported to the airfield for our flight to Oxford. I think that after being told all this, and never having had our feet off the ground before, sleep was very hard to come by. I was thinking what a long way down it was from a plane and were there enough parachutes?!

I think we dozed off and by morning were sleeping quite heavily when someone nearby said it was 06:30. We all sat around wondering what had gone wrong – we even checked we had the right day! The sergeant came in smiling and said, "You lucky buggers - the Japs have surrendered." I have never heard such a cheer before, with men jumping for joy and thinking how lucky they were.

They put on some film shows for us and opened a bar to celebrate. We were allowed to go out into Brussels and join in the celebrations with the Belgian population which went on all day and night.

When we had left Germany for Belgium we were allowed to change only two hundred Deutschmarks into Belgian francs. As Charlie and I had no marks to exchange, Johnny Goodson, who had a lot of marks left over, gave us both two hundred marks to change at the pay office for him. So on this night of joy and celebration, Johnny, with a large sum of francs in his pocket, said he'd take us for a night on the town!

We made our way through the crowds of civilians and soldiers to the centre of Brussels, which was alive with music and everyone enjoying themselves. Johnny found a restaurant with a running cabaret show and led the way in. However, the waiter who met us said that there was no more room. The three of us stood there looking forlorn and thinking that we'd better try elsewhere when a man came towards us and shook our hands. He invited us to sit at his table, telling the waiter to bring three chairs for the English soldiers. We followed him right down to the front of the stage – we couldn't believe our luck! Johnny ordered some wine and we toasted our army, the Belgian army and Monty, who they thought had saved Brussels from the German army when they broke through in the Ardennes.

The show began with a comedian speaking in French, so we cheered and clapped with the crowd to give the impression that we understood the jokes! He was followed by a Belgian girl singing the old favourites like 'Lili Marlene,' a few songs that we knew the tune but not the words, and finishing with "Au Revoir." Johnny kept our drinks topped up and Charlie and I were quite happily enjoying the show, the finale of which was the Can-Can, which somehow developed into a striptease, which was loudly applauded! Saying goodbye to our host and hostess and thanking them, we made our way back to our billets, all holding on to each other with Johnny in the middle. We made it back OK and lay in our beds, thinking what a great way to finish World War II.

Within the week we had moved to the small town of Olsene, which is about twelve miles south of Ghent on the N43, where we were to stay for the next month. We would be billeted with civilians and I was sent with Freddy Illing to number 42 on the main road. When we found the house it had a shop selling photographic items, with a studio on the first floor. Later we were shown round a printing press which was on the ground floor. We were met by Elodie Cuyper and her husband Jozef and welcomed to their home. We were shown to a bedroom to the rear of the house and left to unpack our kit and sample the beds, which after the hard floors of Brussels were luxury indeed! We were told that dinner would be ready in an hour and was being prepared in the school building. Freddy and I had a walk around to get our bearings and found Charlie had been billeted in a room above a café – how lucky can you get!

We had our meal and were washing our mess tins, when the cook-corporal came by and asked if anyone was interested in doing duties with him. Thinking of the food that might be left buckshee after serving the company, I said I was willing to give it a try. I had to make an early start as breakfast was to be at 08:00 and there was a shortage of bread, so I had to cut a hundred and forty very thin slices of bread to make them go round! After dishing up the meal and tidying up, the dixies had to be kept shining so that you could see your face in them. If you succeeded in doing this, you had a meal when you had finished. As I was leaving the cook told me that I would be excused guard duties. This made my day and I stayed with that job until we left for the Middle East in four or five weeks' time.

It was during our stay in Olsene that we were told what our next role was to be. The 3rd Division was to move to the Middle East and keep watch in that troubled land, doing distinctly unglamorous tasks like guarding deserted streets and making cordons while the police went in to do their armed searches.

Leave started again with forty-eight hour leave passes to Blankenberge on the coast, where I went with Shuff (Shufflebottom) and Mac (MacNulty). My nickname throughout the time I was in the army was Joe - Joe Soap perhaps! Back in Olsene we were shown round the printing side of the business. Georges showed me how he worked the machine, which was made in England and was "very good OK." He also said he liked our cigarettes which we used to give to him. Time went very quickly in this friendly place and two or three days before we were due to leave we were invited by Gabriel to dinner one evening at his house which was away from the main road. Freddy and I walked along the track to Gabriel's house and were met by our host and his wife Yvonne and other friends. We had a lovely meal with wine and were sorry when it was time to go. Walking back with Freddy, we felt sorry to be leaving Olsene, but were still looking forward to our voyage to Palestine and Egypt. For many years I kept in touch with the family through Yvonne.

October came and we were due to move the next day, so we had our photos taken in the studio. I took a photo with my camera of Freddy,

Elodie, Jozef and Gabriel, and someone I have no recollection of took a picture of the five of us. The day came for the trucks to pick us up and I can vividly remember Elodie saying goodbye to us with tears in her eyes.

We boarded the train in Boulogne or Dieppe and I really enjoyed the journey. The French railways were all electric, so there was no fear of bits in your eyes as there was with steam, and we soon picked up speed. The scenery was constantly changing, but after an hour I think most of us had nodded off! After seven hours or more the train slowed down and moved into some sidings. Everyone was ordered out and marched to a rather large building where a meal had been prepared for us, our last before Toulon. The stop here lasted about an hour and I think they gave us a haversack ration to keep us going until we arrived at camp. At last we were marched back to the train and so moved on to the second part of our journey to the Mediterranean and beyond. We slept mostly throughout the night and when we awoke in the morning some of us moved our stiff limbs and were rewarded on opening our bleary eyes when we saw in the sunlight that lovely blue of the "Med."

The railway line followed the coast nearly all the way to Toulon and when the train stopped for some reason I had my camera ready for one or two photos. We finally arrived at about midday and were taken straight to the camp, where we enjoyed a good wash and brush up after that very long journey into the warmer weather of southern France. We then went on parade for the issue of bedding for the week until we boarded ship. We took them back to our tents and found them to be filthy, so we had to take them out and give them a good shake. The amount of dust that came out was unbelievable. That night when we settled down I put on my P.T. shorts and kept my shirt on. We had a lovely week there and found a beautiful bay near Hyères-Plage where we went swimming most days in the clear blue water, and where I learnt to swim. The last two days there were spoilt by the Mistral, which is a violent cold, dry north-east wind, which I think travels down the Rhône valley.

Chapter Ten
Palestine and Demob

It was now time for us to leave and, on arriving at the quayside we started to board a lovely looking French boat, named "Villa d'Oran." We were shown to our mess deck, which turned out to be our sleeping quarters and where we slung our hammocks. Charlie decided to hang his near the porthole where we would get a nice breeze blowing through. I hung my hammock on the other side of him, which turned out to be a good move. When we sailed into some rough weather Charlie was thrown against the wing-nuts on the porthole and suffered bruising caused by my hammock! Eventually he stuffed his blanket down his side to ease the pain and was very grateful when we sailed into calmer water.

During this rough spell of weather I didn't feel too good so I decided to look for a place to kip. I found a small theatre which had some sliding doors where the stage was. Behind the doors I found some carpets so I lay down and quickly fell asleep. At 8pm that evening I woke up feeling much better and wandered back to our mess deck where Charlie demanded to know from me where I'd been. He had apparently been quite worried and had been searching for me, even looking in the theatre, but had not seen me as I had closed the sliding doors.

At this time of evening we were passing the small volcanic island of Stromboli, with just a whisper of smoke on the crest, and sailed on towards the Messina Straits. Our approach to the straits was announced on the ship's tannoy and we all went up on deck to see the lights of a little town on the mainland of Italy. It seemed to all of us watching that if the ship kept on the same course we would certainly hit the mainland, but at the last moment when all seemed lost, the ship turned between the town and Messina on the island of Sicily. After passing through the straits we sailed on for two more days before tying up at Port Said, the entrance to the Suez Canal which splits Africa and Asia.

On docking all the Army men on board went on deck to look out on the spectacle of Port Said. Whilst we were leaning on the handrail we could feel the ship moving over and the boat alarms came on. The tannoy instructed us to go immediately to our boat stations. We were told later that all of us going over to one side could have been disastrous, but with everyone going to their boat-stations an even keel was regained once more. I bet the sailors were all glad when we departed!

We were soon disembarked and loaded into trucks which were to take us along a road overlooking the ships on the canal. We were taken to a big army camp overlooking the Bitter Lakes, near Ismailia. At this point the ships wait in the lakes to await their turn to progress through the canal. The camp had an open-air cinema nearby, a football stadium, a beach where we could swim and showers to wash the salt off after.

We unloaded all our kit and were marched off to a tented area, where we had camp beds and a large tin box to keep our personal things in and it also kept out the desert sand. There were eight men to a tent and we all had mosquito nets which had to be put up every evening without fail. After we had settled in, we were called out to go to the store to get issued with our shorts, and when we paraded with them on, everybody fell about laughing at our fat, thin and hairy legs. We had a NAAFI which provided canteen facilities and after our first hot day which was around 90 to 100 degrees we were ready for a nice cold beer. This was Canadian bottled beer and after two or three Charlie and I were ready to "hit the hay." We were told that reveille would be at five so we could service the carriers and do other jobs before the sun got too hot, and hats should be worn at all times. We lay on the top of our beds, most with just our P.T. shorts on and quickly fell asleep – it had been a long day! Most of us were woken up around midnight shivering with cold and quickly pulled our blankets back on top of us, not realising that the temperature drops very rapidly in the desert.

Morning came very soon and the air was lovely and cool while we washed and shaved, and after breakfast we started to service the carriers. As the sun rose and got higher, the metal on the carrier and spanners was burning our hands, and our feet in our army boots were quite warm to say the least.

At around ten we were off duty for the rest of the day and spent most of our time on the beach and in the water to keep cool. We had been warned that anyone who reported sick with sunstroke would be put on a charge, so most of us always had a handkerchief tied around our necks which gave us some protection.

A few days later we were warned of an approaching sand-storm that would reach our area around evening time. We were told to get our shovels and dig a trench around the tent and pile it up around the canvas to stop it blowing away, and lower the flaps on the window openings and tie securely. All this preparation made us feel a little uneasy, not knowing quite what was going to hit us! There was an escarpment to the west of us about two miles away and after three or four hours the wind began to pick up and dark clouds formed over it. Within the hour the sky had darkened and we then thought it was time to get inside and tie down the door flaps. The wind and the sand had come and the noise was devastating as we lay on our beds expecting to see the tent depart into the sky. But the work we had done in the afternoon held it firm and after a while we were more relaxed and started preparing to get to sleep. We lowered our mosquito nets and tried, but it took a long time. The wind did die down a little so we did manage to nod off eventually.

By morning the sandstorm had passed and when reveille was blown, I started to sit upright in bed and where my head had been lying on my pillow was clean, but all round it was this very fine sand which had been filtered through the fine mesh of the mosquito net.

Most of us had sand in our hair, noses and ears and were glad to get an early wash and shave. Breakfast was taken and we spent the day tidying up after the night's storm, and those who were down for guard duties in the evening cleaned their equipment ready for inspection. On guard at night you had to patrol right round the camp, an area of a mile or so, and it was difficult to maintain vigil especially during the hours of darkness, and so a lot of thefts were reported. Most of it disappeared into the night, taken by the local inhabitants. It was rumoured that the thieves took an officers' tent down while they slept and took it away – and other things - and they only found out when they were awakened by the cold night air, and the stars shining down upon them. Charlie and I were glad that we were not on guard duty that night!

After two or more weeks we were on the road again, which was to take us into the troubles that were happening in Palestine. We crossed the Suez Canal and into the Sinai desert and through the Negeb to a large Army camp near to the town of Hadera where we would stay for the next six months. We were glad to wash and clean ourselves up after a tiring and dusty journey. We were then summoned on parade to be told that the camp was enclosed in three coils of barbed wire with mines placed in the centre of the wire and that guards would patrol the camp at all times. We should when required help the police in hunting out arms caches and terrorists, who at the moment were blowing up Coastguard stations and Army transport when they had the chance. Not a happy state of affairs, we thought. Not all was gloom and doom as we were right in the middle of the orange growing area, and the owner said that we could help ourselves to as many as we wanted provided we did not damage the trees. We took it in turns to take a kit bag and fill it with lovely Jaffa oranges, if you remembered to pick the ripe ones!

Also outside the perimeter fence were some stables where they kept four or five horses for the officers to ride and were looked after by an ex-guardsman, who when in England had cared for some of the horses at Windsor Castle. They were beautiful Arab horses and while I was admiring them, he suddenly said that he would bring one out to let me ride on. By the time he had brought it out from the stable, there was still a look of horror on my face. "There's nothing to it," he said and with that he grabbed my leg and before I knew where I was, I sat astride the horse with no reins to hold on to – only the horse's mane. I must admit the horse stood very still and I know that I sat very still. I felt that if I let go of its mane I would slide off its bare back, and it looked a long way down to the ground. The chap then slapped the horse's rear end and told me to move off, and I did, right over the horse's head and into a wadi which was close by. Picking myself up and dusting myself down, I climbed out. My friend laughed and said, "Let's try it again." I thanked him and said, "I think once is enough. I am on guard duty in ten minutes," and hurried back to camp.

What I liked about Palestine was that the weather was warm but not like the excessive heat of Egypt. What they called winter here was about four weeks overcast and not a lot of rain and still very pleasant.

After a short time we were called on to throw a cordon around the town of Hadera while the police went in to do their armed searches, looking for terrorists and arms buried in the sand or houses. The coastguard stations also were attacked with one or two being wrecked, and we had to be on our guard. When we had some time off two or three mortar carriers would go to the beaches and we would have enjoyable afternoons swimming and getting a tan, but always with two men on guard and keeping very alert.

We had been in camp for two or three months and my mate Charlie said that there was a truck going into Haifa, so we decided to go with about twelve other soldiers, all carrying rifles to be on the safe side. When we arrived Charlie and I headed for the Y.M.C.A. which we knew served up some nice meals, and we were feeling hungry. Most of the others had gone off for a pint or two. When we had finished our meal we had a game of table tennis and had a nap in the easy chairs. We left to go back to where the lorry would leave from, to find that we were the only two there. The driver arrived and said he knew where all the others were - mostly "under the weather" with a drop too much to drink! So we helped the driver to coax them back to the lorry and the ones who felt sick were sat on the back seats so that we kept the lorry clean – if possible. I think we were glad to get back to camp that night without losing anybody over the tail-board.

While we were in Palestine, all the old soldiers who had been called up in 1939 were due to be released and I said goodbye to my old number one Johnny Goodson and Frank Dickenson.   I took a photograph of them standing outside the tent, and then they were on their way back to England. I felt sad at their parting. They had been a lot longer in the fighting than me, and being in the phoney war in 1940 and Dunkirk were lucky to have made it. (In 1983 while on holiday in Skegness with my wife Audrey, I finally met Frank at his farm at Gosberton Fen, where we were made welcome by his wife Eileen).

With the parting of the older soldiers, we found out that we became the "old hands" and promotion was in the offing. Charlie became a Lance Corporal (one stripe) and I was offered the same, but after a lot of persuasion by Charlie I still said no and remained a Private until I left the Army in July 1946.

A week after Charlie's promotion, he was in charge of the guard at a place called Pardes Hanna, set on a hillside away from our main camp and among an orchard of eucalyptus trees. I did not know what trees they were until I touched one of the flower buds, which were sticky and also had a very strong smell.

When we had unpacked our equipment and moved into a building which was our guard-room, "Lance Corporal Smith" had the guard on parade for inspection and to read the guards' orders out to us. Charlie gave me everything: "Get your hair cut! If it gets any longer you will trip over it," and a few other things. He then read the roster out at what times we should be on duty. I think I finished with the 4am till 6am duty when you feel sleepy and cold while the dawn breaks and two hours seem like four!

When we arrived back we were still pals and we had a good laugh with Charlie remarking, "I always wanted that feeling of power over you lot!"

We left for Egypt on a hot dusty day in convoy, the three-ton trucks all leaving behind the air full of arid dust from the Sinai desert. After about a two hour drive and with dusk fast approaching, we finally stopped where the cooks, who had gone before us, had set up their burners and had a hot meal waiting for the convoy to arrive. That stew and a mug of tea to wash the dust out of our throats were luxury indeed! We stopped there for the night and slept (if we could) under the stars, but the ground was very stony, and if you slept on your blanket you were no better off. When the heat of the day had gone the night turned very cold, so the blankets had to be used over our "greatcoats" to achieve some semblance of warmth. The cooks awoke before dawn and made breakfast so that the convoy would get away before the sun rose. We packed our equipment onto our lorry, still feeling stiff and cold, and moved towards the Suez Canal and back to our base near the Bitter Lakes.

On arriving back we had the choice of seven days' leave in Cairo or Alexandria. Charlie said that Cairo would be unbearable in the heat, whereas Alexandria on the coast would have a nice cool breeze. We arrived in "Alex" on the 21st November 1945 and went to the St Andrews Hostel where we signed in for seven days and paid a hundred and forty piastre for bed and breakfast – room 14 and bed number 61 (yes, I kept the receipt!). Our main meal was taken in a restaurant nearby where the food was OK but not a lot of it. When we did venture out we were pestered all the time by shoe-shine boys, which was most annoying. One morning we decided to walk to the sea front which we found very dirty (no deck chairs!), so we carried on along the road, when out of nowhere there were two or three shoe-shine boys after us. We kept saying no, but that did not deter them. They then tried to wet our boots on the toe cap, which dulled the shine so they hoped that we would ask them to shine it up again. Charlie's boots were immaculate and his pride and joy, so when this boy tried to wet his boot Charlie stamped down so hard on his wrist that he yelled out with pain. We left them and quickly made our way back to the main road where our hostel was. Halfway back I looked over my shoulder and about two hundred yards behind were these three lads shouting and waving their arms. They had been joined by two fellows who looked about six foot tall and rather menacing. Charlie took one look and we both ran like hell and we were glad when we turned the corner and found our billet. We had a good rest but I think we were glad to get back to the Bitter Lakes.

Charlie and I both used to talk about which of us would get out of the Army first. I said that I was a bricklayer, so would be the one to go. Charlie said he worked in a factory which made metal windows which would be needed first. We were both hoping to get out under the Class "B" release system.

After I had been back a week I was sent on a driver-mechanic course with two others (one I think was called Alf Cook) to an airfield on the side of the Suez Canal, and someone took a photograph of the two of us standing there. Behind us an aircraft carrier was moving up the Canal, bringing back troops from the Far East.

The course was for six weeks and when I arrived back at camp and went to my tent and looked for Charlie, I then noticed that his kit was gone and there was an empty bed. I found that he had left for Blighty two or three days before. The next day I had to go to company office and was told I was on L.I.A.P. leave to England for four weeks. I packed my overseas kitbag and all my equipment and was taken to Alexandria where I boarded the "Staffordshire" to Toulon.

We set sail around midday under a clear blue sky that stayed with us all the way back, with the sea as calm as a mill pond and a journey to enjoy. We stopped at Malta in the Grand Harbour to pick up mail and also deliver some. I took time to stand and look at this small island and reflect what trauma it had been subjected to during the war, and what might have been if Malta had fallen. After a short stay we sailed out of the Grand Harbour and continued our journey to Toulon, passing the islands of Sardinia and Corsica on the way. After docking we disembarked and boarded the train which would take us right through to Calais. Here we embarked on a Liberty ship - an American ship which was mass-produced and had a flat bottom, no keel, and was filled with concrete to try and give it some stability in rough seas, and why most people travelling on it were usually sea-sick!

What most of us wanted to see were the lovely white cliffs and green fields which seemed to say welcome home. After disembarking at Dover we had to pass through Customs, and we had been warned that if we were caught bringing in anything illegally we would forfeit our leave and be sent straight back to our base in Egypt. When you pass through customs, you have that feeling of "have I anything in my kit bag which I should have declared?" and a great feeling of relief when you arrive on the other side without being stopped.

I finally arrived in Desborough six hours later at the station, and only had a short distance to carry all my kit to 58 Queen Street, where my dear old mother greeted me with a hug and a kiss, being quite surprised to see me. So I explained everything which had happened so quickly with the leave pass and that if I had written a letter, I would have arrived before the letter. Dad arrived later from Storefield signal box, and proceeded to play his latest chant on the piano to me!

Time passed quickly and out of the blue I received a letter from the Army, offering me the chance of a Class "B" release, and being a bricklayer it was to help start the building industry up after all the years of war.

I wrote and accepted it, and was sent a train pass for Beverley which was the No.5 Holding Battalion of the Lincolns. I travelled by train via Nottingham, Doncaster and Hull arriving in Beverley around lunchtime and walked the mile or so to the barracks which was just outside the town, passing the lovely cathedral on the way. Presenting my pass at the guardroom I was shown my sleeping quarters and joined the others who were on demob. Later on we were given a check over by the Medical Officer to see if we were fit to leave the Army!

The next morning we had to go in front of the Company Officer who would sign our final release. I walked in and sat down on a chair in front of him thinking that my Army days were over, when he shouted out "Don't you usually salute an officer?" stating to me that "it's not too late to be put on a charge!" I said nothing and just sat there while he wrote out my release which he handed to me. I felt a lot better with that in my hand and then I stood up and made a move to leave when he bellowed out again, "I have to write a reference about your Army record before you leave." I replied that he need not bother, as I had already a job waiting for me and left the room. The other men who went for the de-mob passes said that he was like that with most of them.

A truck was then laid on to take us to York to the demob centre where they held all the clothing - suit, shirt, shoes etc. We were handed out different things and then moved down to where the suits were, and a soldier told me the size that would fit me and gave me the patter - this dark blue suit would be the one for me. I said no, there were some racks further on that I wanted to look round and the soldier seemed determined to keep me away from. I found what I wanted - a brown suit which had been hidden right at the back of the racks. He came rushing along again trying to put me off, saying that it would not fit. Not to be deterred, I tried it on and it fitted OK, with the soldier looking as mad as a hatter. We found out later that they kept them out of the way for officers who would tip them, and they were making a "bob or two" on the side. He was a bit short on the day I came! We carried all our kit to the end of the building where it was all packed into a box, and off we went to the truck which would be returning to Beverley. As the truck turned into the road the spiv boys were waiting for us, offering a fiver for the boxes with all our kit in. They say that a soldier took a suitcase with him and put all his demob stuff in it, kept the empty box tied up with string and when the spiv offered him a fiver, which he took, he then threw the box out of the lorry. When he went to pick it up he knew he had been had! We arrived back at the barracks and picked up our kit which we were allowed to take with us, and the truck took us to the station where we said goodbyes and all went our different ways. The date was 13th July 1946.

Travelling back home on the train and reading my Class "B" release papers, it stated that I was released on 13th July 1946 for an indefinite period. Before I started work I had to go to the Labour Exchange in Gold Street (now Marlow House) to a Mr Ireson with my release papers. He told me to report to H. Martin, a building firm from Northampton, who were building pre-fabs in Highfield Road, Kettering.

On my first day of work I had to catch the 7 o'clock bus, and I had a long walk to the site where I met the foreman who teamed me with another "brickie" and a labourer. Bending my back doing the footings and completing them in a day, I was glad when the whistle blew at 4.30 pm so I could catch the bus home. After dinner I was so tired and ready for bed very early in the evening.

I lasted out for four weeks and the brickwork was finished when the site foreman informed me that the next job was in Northampton and would I like to go there? I replied that I was hopeful of getting back to work in Desborough, and so he gave me a form which released me. I took this to the Labour Office in Kettering and was allowed to go back to the firm I originally worked for.

This is the end of my story of a journey which lasted four and a half years and took me to Scotland, France, Belgium, Holland and Germany, across the Mediterranean Sea to Egypt and Palestine and I wonder how many miles?

My wife Audrey and our children, David, Barbara and Jennifer met on holidays with Charlie and Mary, Alan, Ronald and Liz a few times, and Charlie was best man at our wedding. I was hoping that when retirement came along we would make time to meet again and talk about the old days, but it was not to be. I had a letter from Mary saying that Charlie had died in August 1987.

THE END

Appendix One

Maps – UK, Caen area and Northern Europe

TRAINING AND PREPARATIONS FOR D-DAY 1942 - 1944

Culbin Sands - Dec 1943

Beauly - Autunm 1943

Isle of Rhum - Autumn 1943

Glenborrodale - Jul 1943

Beinn Resipol - Autumn 1943

Inverary - Jun 1943

Kyles of Bute - Autumn 1943

Hawick 1944

GREAT BRITAIN

Norwich - Aug 1942

Desborough

Hythe - May 1943

Portsmouth - Apr 1944

Newquay - Jan 1943

6 Jun 1944

FRANCE

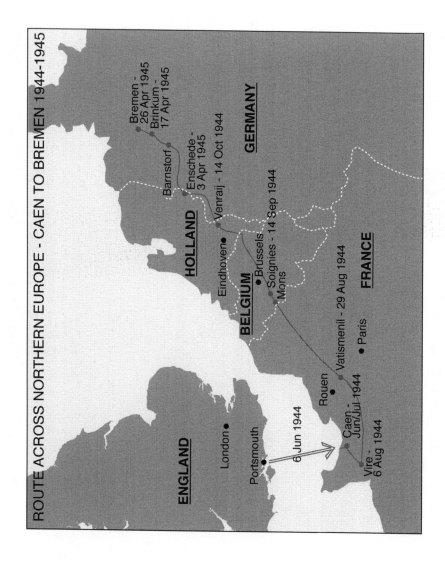

ROUTE ACROSS NORTHERN EUROPE - CAEN TO BREMEN 1944-1945

Bremen -
26 Apr 1945
Brinkum -
17 Apr 1945

Barnstorf

Enschede -
3 Apr 1945

Venraij - 14 Oct 1944

GERMANY

HOLLAND

Eindhoven

Brussels

Soignies - 14 Sep 1944

Mons

BELGIUM

Vatismenil - 29 Aug 1944

Paris

FRANCE

Rouen

Caen -
Jun/Jul 1944

Vire -
6 Aug 1944

ENGLAND

London

Portsmouth

6 Jun 1944

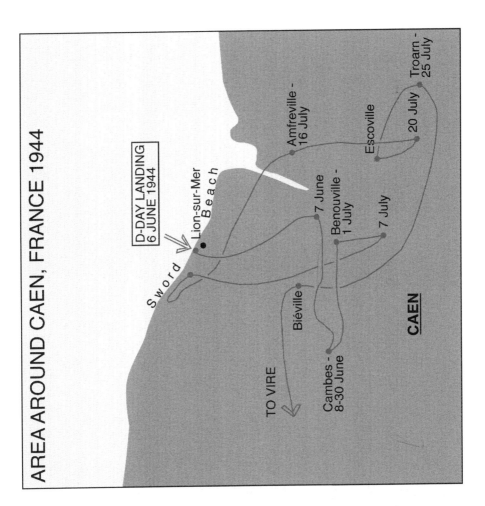

AREA AROUND CAEN, FRANCE 1944

D-DAY LANDING
6 JUNE 1944

Lion-sur-Mer

Beach

Sword

Amfreville -
16 July

Escoville

20 July

Troarn -
25 July

7 June

Benouville -
1 July

7 July

Biéville

Cambes -
8-30 June

TO VIRE

CAEN

Appendix Two
Medical Call-up Paper
11 June 1942

NATIONAL SERVICE ACTS, 1939 to 1941

MINISTRY OF LABOUR AND NATIONAL SERVICE

Local Office.....................NORTHAMPTON

Registration No. DFZ-1654.   11·6·42   (Date)

> Mr. Raymond C. Paine
> 58. Queen Street
> Desborough.
> Northants

DEAR SIR,

I have to inform you that in accordance with the National Service Acts you are required to submit yourself to medical examination by a medical board at 8·30 a.m. on TUESDAY day, 16 JUN 1942 194....., at the Medical Board Centre, THE DOVER HALL ST. JAMES, NORTHAMPTON

If you wear glasses, you should bring them with you to the Medical Board.

On reporting for medical examination you should present this form and your Certificate of Registration (N.S. 2 or N.S.62) to the clerk in charge of the waiting room.

*A Travelling Warrant for your return journey is enclosed. Before starting your journey you must exchange the warrant for a ticket at the booking office named on the warrant. You should take special care of the return half of the ticket as in the event of loss you will be required to obtain a fresh ticket at normal fare at your own expense.

*If you reside more than six miles from the Medical Board Centre and travel by omnibus or tram your fare will be paid at the Centre.

Any expenses or allowances which may become payable to you in accordance with the scale overleaf will be paid to you on application when you attend at the Medical Board Centre.

Immediately on receipt of this notice, you should inform your employer of the date and time at which you are required to attend for medical examination.

If you are called up you will receive a further notification giving you at least three days' notice. You should accordingly not voluntarily give up your employment because you are required to attend for medical examination.

Your attention is directed to the Notes printed on the back of this Notice.

Yours faithfully,

J. E. POTT

N.S.6
*Delete if not applicable.   Manager.   (P.T.O.

Appendix Three
Army Release Paper
13 July 1946

WARNING:—It is most important that this form should not be lost, as no duplicate will be issued.

Army Form W.3044
(in pads of 25)

Serial No.

RELEASE OF SOLDIER TO CLASS W., ROYAL ARMY RESERVE, OR TO CLASS W. (T) T.A. RESERVE, OR OF AUXILIARY TO A.T.S. UNEMPLOYED LIST

A 442954

THIS IS TO CERTIFY that No. *14216788* Rank *PTE*

Name : *PAINE R.C.*

Unit *No. 5 INF. HOLDING BN. LINCOLNS.* has been

relegated to* { Class W., Royal Army Reserve
Class W. (T) T.A. Reserve
Unemployed List, A.T.S. *Solu2.*

* { for a definite period
or
for an indefinite period } from *13/7/46* to *INDEFINITE*

Wood Capt LT. COL.
Commanding

O.C. No. 5 INF. HOLDING BN.

(Space for Unit's stamp)

INFANTRY HOLDING BATTALION 13/7/46

Station *BEVERLEY*

* Delete whichever is inapplicable.
(GV701) Wt.32170/3763. 5,850 Bks. 11/44. B. & S. Ltd 51-846.

Date *13/7/46.*

(See NOTICE at back.)

- 83 -

Appendix Four
Record of Service
23 July 1946

Record Office Stamp	RECORD OF SERVICE	ARMY FORM W5258
23 JUL 1946 YORK	OF No. 14216788 Rank Pte	4
	Name PRINE R.C. (in block letters)	

Served in Regts/Corps as follows :

(2024) Wt.16031 Dd6234 350m (15) 7/45 Gp.697 C&SLtd

	Regt./Corps	From	To	Assn. joined with date	Remarks by Assn. (if any)
a	GSC	16·6·42	15·9·42		
b	NORTHANTS	16·9·42	25·2·43		
c	LINCS R	26·2·43	3·8·44		
d					

Date 23·7·46 .... Record Officer

1. This card should be presented or sent by the person named above to the Regt/Corps Association he wishes to join or from which he requires assistance.
2. The Secretary of the Association should stamp and date the card in the relative column when the soldier joins the Association.

Appendix Five
Barbara's Poem 2005

When you see this shadow of my former self
Dependent on carers, poor in health
Go back sixty-one years to a Normandy shore
To a fit young man, one of many at war.
Remember now when I can't walk, sing or dance
I ran and fought on those beaches in France.
When I'm deaf and I cannot hear very well
And you have to repeat all that you tell
Guns deafened my hearing in World War Two
Now it's a difficult task to understand you.
When it takes me a while to absorb what you say
Recall my alertness on that memorable day.
When I can't read print and images are unsure
Remember the things that these tired eyes once saw
Guns firing, shells bursting ending so many lives
Lost friends who would never return to their wives
When I'm confused and can't cope with the things of today
The brave friends I lost seem to join me and say
"Don't worry Ray you still have a great life
With caring friends, a family and wife.
On those D-Day beaches I was merely a boy
I fought for a future for you all to enjoy
You are that future, so live life to the full
And remember Ray Paine – Unforgettable.

Poem written by Barbara Crowther   2005

Bibliography and Acknowledgements

The main source that my father appears to have referenced in writing this account is a pamphlet written during and soon after the events of 1944-45. It is titled "The History of the Second Battalion the Lincolnshire Regiment in North-West Europe – Hermanville-sur-Mer 6 June 1944 to Lengerich 8 May 1945." There is no author listed, no publisher and no date. This appears to be a primary source and is acknowledged as such by the inclusion of the following paragraph in the foreword : "This narrative is intended as a guide in conjunction with the official War Diary for the use of whoever may undertake the compilation of a History of the Regiment during the present war."

I must thank Patrick Delaforce, the author of Monty's Ironsides and also his publishers, Alan Sutton Publishing Ltd. My father provided Patrick with photographs and written material which were both used in the book. Some information from Patrick's book is referred to in my father's memoirs.

Every effort has been made to identify the source of the material that my father referenced to fill in the gaps in his narrative in order to put his experiences into the wider context of the northern Europe campaign. His descent into Alzheimers over the past eight years has made it impossible to ask him for his sources. Where it has not been possible to contact copyright owners I extend my apologies and thank them for their contribution to this account.

Dave Paine 2013

Index